**Maurizio Terzini** was born in Melbourne to Italian parents, Gina and Arnaldo. When Maurizio was nine years old his family returned to live in Pescara, a small city on Italy's Adriatic Coast, where they stayed for five years. During this time he developed a passion for his Italian heritage, particularly the Italians' love of food, sharing meals, hospitality and conversation.

The Terzini family came back to Melbourne in 1980. In 1988 Maurizio opened his first cafe, the much-loved Caffé e Cucina, in Chapel Street, South Yarra. Since then, Maurizio has revolutionised modern Australian dining in Melbourne and Sydney, creating some of Australia's most successful cafes, bars and restaurants, which have set a benchmark for impeccable and relaxed dining around the country.

Maurizio lives in Sydney with his partner, Kirrily, and has a son, Sylvester. Maurizio's current passion and project is Icebergs Dining Room and Bar, at Bondi Beach.

# Maurizio Terzini

# Something Italian

Photography by David Matheson

Drawings by David Band

LANTERN
*an imprint of*
PENGUIN BOOKS

## DEDICATION

I would like to dedicate this book to my family. To my father, Arnaldo: I consider myself very lucky that we could work together for so many years. To my mother, Gina: thank you for the simple flavours I will treasure forever. Thank you both for being proud to be Italian and for teaching me to be proud to be an Italo-Australian. To my brother, Marco, and my sister, Lisa: thank you for your love and support.

To my son, Sylvester: without your love, friendship and understanding I would not have the strength that I have today to continue working and enjoying my work.

# Contents

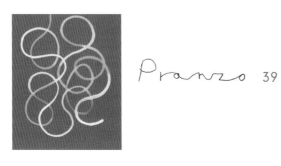

# From Pescara to South Yarra to Bondi

When you read this book, I want you to feel that you are experiencing something personal and special, which is also how I want you to feel when you come into one of my restaurants.

My philosophy on food and service draws very much on my family background and experiences. I was born in Melbourne but when I was nine my family returned to live in Pescara, a small city in Abruzzo in central Italy, and my memories of food and sharing meals in Italy have greatly influenced the style of food I serve in my restaurants. Our day in Italy was very structured and ritualised, and was dominated by food, so the recipes in this book are grouped together to represent those times of the day when we ate: *colazione* (breakfast), *aperitivo* (late-morning drink and snack), *pranzo* (lunch), *spuntino* (afternoon snack), *cena* (dinner), *dolce* (dessert) and *mezzanotte* (late-night snack). Sharing a meal was always a social event.

Pescara was a classic Italian town: large enough to be a metropolis but small enough to be social, intimate and very conservative. In Italy my family only ate out on special occasions – baptisms, communions and weddings – and it was always lunch, rarely dinner. Each summer, we would spend a few weeks in both my mother's and my father's villages just outside of Pescara, not far from where we lived. My mother, Gina, grew up in Abbateggio, and my father, Arnaldo, grew up just 15 kilometres away in Tocco da Casauria (although they didn't meet until after they both moved to Australia in the 1950s). During those summer holidays we would occasionally eat out in one of the local *trattorie*. It was nothing like dining out in Australia; there was no menu. There was just one woman cooking pasta, and when it came time to order, she would ask how many people wanted gnocchi and we would put our hands up, then she would ask how many wanted tortellini, and so on. While she was cooking the pasta, the antipasto platters loaded with local meats and cheeses would come out. We wouldn't be offered any choice; everything was just simple and fresh. There were no overloaded menus, no entrée-main-and-dessert structure adhered to. All the food came out at once, and it always felt like home. To me, that's the best kind of experience, and I have always tried to bring to my restaurants and cafes that feeling of being able to drop in at any time and have a plate of pasta, an aperitif or something sweet.

Pescara was small enough to maintain many old traditions. Every afternoon, we would finish siesta (siesta was taken seriously in my home town; we weren't allowed to play soccer in the street or go downstairs or make any noise, and if we did we had things thrown at us from the apartments above) – and then we would head down to the *piazza* in town to hang out. We began socialising independently by the time we were thirteen or fourteen, and we had to pick which group we would socialise with, whether it was a political association, a fashion association or a cultural association. Though our city was very conservative, we were living through a cultural revolution of sorts. The central *piazza* was split down the middle by the main road, and each side represented a different political affiliation; you had to choose very early on which side of the *piazza* was your side. It was a melting pot of passion and politics.

My family came back to Australia when I was fifteen, but when I was twenty I returned to Italy for a year. During this time I fell in love with the Italian cafe scene, which was so different from anything in Australia, and I wanted to bring a little part of it to Melbourne. I wanted to share the age-old Italian philosophy of service: no matter whether you order a cup of coffee or a three-course meal, you receive the same impeccable quality of service. Back in the 1980s, this philosophy wasn't seen in Melbourne, particularly in cafes, and I wanted to change that.

When I finished school, I was lucky enough to become part of the Fitzroy scene, working in cafes and clubs. During the 1980s I worked at Vic Ave, Black Cat cafe and Mario's. I learnt an incredible amount about the industry, with my time at Mario's probably having the strongest influence on me at that stage in my life. At the time, I felt that the style of Italian food being served in most restaurants was too commercial and didn't reflect what I had experienced in Italy.

When I started planning my first cafe, I had not done an apprenticeship, nor had any formal training. My father, Arnaldo Terzini, had owned a bar in Pescara, and he taught me the most essential thing about service: patience. My father would never say no to business, no matter how many people kept coming into his bar.

Hanging out in Pescara, Italy, 1985

Arnaldo Terzini, Caffé e Cucina, 1989

Maurizio and Arnaldo, 1992

I started with the notion of a little contemporary cafe that would let people step out of Melbourne and into Italy for a while; somewhere I could create a mix of Italy and Australia. I also knew that I had to adapt my ideas about Italian food for the Australian market. I wanted my clients to come into my place and feel special, feel a part of it. I had particular ideas about food, service, design and table settings, and I poured all my plans into my first cafe.

It took me two and a half years to find the perfect site for Caffé e Cucina. Chapel Street, South Yarra, was worlds away from Carlton, which had always been the traditional home of 'Little Italy', and that was exactly what I wanted. In those days, South Yarra was nothing like it is today. The site was surrounded by factories, the old pub, plus a few funky streetwear stores, but otherwise there was nothing there.

In 1988 I, together with my first business partner, Maria, my cousin Anthony and our families, took over an old restaurant, a tiny space crammed in among shopfronts. We wanted to pour some soul into it. Under the guidance of designer Chris Connell, we built Caffé e Cucina almost from scratch. We stripped concrete, we cleaned, we repaired tiles, we re-upholstered old furniture, we re-tiled the kitchen, we stained the walls, we prepared the floors. My uncle painted, and my father helped in so many ways to get us through. The name of our place – Caffé e Cucina – really said what our place was all about: coffee and cooking.

We didn't have much space or money, but I knew that the most important thing we needed was the right style and atmosphere – something modern, Italian and a little bohemian. The atmosphere we created – the vases, the lampshades, the prints, the bottles, the Italian biscuit tins – is intact today and is, I think, why so many people love Caffé e Cucina. Our regular clients became our friends, and no-one seemed to mind having to sit at the bar and wait for an hour to get a table, or that our menu was only written in Italian. Our clients loved hearing the staff shout to each other in Italian as they rushed around, squeezing between tables and people; there was never much room to move around, but that added to the atmosphere. I wanted people to talk, to laugh, to shout. I never wanted the service or the food to

Chris Connell's vision for Caffé e Cucina

Opening year at Caffé e Cucina, 1988

interrupt the conversation or experience; they should always complement the social gathering. We kept the lighting low and discreet so people felt that they were stepping into something intimate, something that transported them away from the rest of the world.

We started with a simple concept of breakfast, lunch and dinner, and we believed that serving the right food for the right time of day was essential; from the beautiful little pastries we displayed in the front window (my mother and my aunt Lidia made all our pastries for the first two years) to the all-day breakfast, and pasta until eleven o'clock at night.

We employed strong principles about quality and service. On opening night I had two waiters working on the floor with me, and together we looked after 65 people. We wore formal uniforms, which was a very Italian thing to do, and we were the first cafe to bring out the Italian white jackets from Italy. At the time, most of the local cafes didn't offer this level of service, or a decent cup of coffee, so we tried to raise the standard for cafe dining while keeping everything affordable and simple.

Our table settings were plain, almost bare, and my philosophy on these has not changed. I love simplicity, and I didn't want anything to get in the way of our clients having a special experience, so we pared back the tables to necessities. There was also space to consider. The bread-and-butter plates were crowding the table, so we took them off. We had a very tight space to work in, so we used small rectangular tables, inside and out, and we designed them to fit the space. I wanted people to be able to sit close together, touch shoulders, laugh and flirt.

I have always tried to encourage my clients to choose the kind of eating experience they will have. Our price range and attitude has always allowed this, even now at Icebergs in Sydney. Our clients might come in at nine o'clock in the evening for a plate of pasta and a glass of wine, and be gone by ten, or they

might come in with their family and friends for an extended dining experience. And they will, I hope, receive the same level of service regardless of what they order and how much money they spend.

The people who first came to Caffé e Cucina were young, hippyish and a little bohemian. We attracted well-travelled people, especially those who had spent a lot of time in Europe, and I think that when they walked into Caffé e Cucina they felt like they were back in Europe. We developed a loyal following, probably because we had broken the mould and started something fresh and new, and we were proud to be second-generation Italians living in Australia.

When we opened Caffé e Cucina, a lot of people thought we were a little radical, which is exactly what we wanted to be. We received criticism from the old guard, who suggested that the 'cafe society' we were encouraging was destroying fine dining, but we maintained our style and eventually won them over.

We set a very basic, good-value menu – we started with four entrées and four main courses, and this is still the case today – and avoided the clichéd mixed-pasta plates. Our menu size was also determined by the size of our kitchen – it was tiny. All we had was an eight-burner stove that we had reconditioned. So, day after day and night after night we turned out meals from our tiny kitchen with one stove.

We served coffee the real Italian way. For the first few years, 20 per cent of our coffees were sent back because customers thought they weren't hot enough, but we persisted and people began to appreciate what we were doing. These days, you can get a great cup of coffee anywhere in Melbourne, but that wasn't the case back then.

One of the keys to our success was the fact that we didn't try to reinvent Italian food. We cooked very simple Italian food that doesn't go out of fashion – I have served some of the recipes in this book for fifteen years, and they are still popular. I don't believe that in Australia you will ever have 100 per cent

authentic Italian food – you can't, because the way Italians eat and consume their food and alcohol is so different to the traditions in Australia – but we did our best to share our experiences of Italian food and culture with the Australian market.

I met Robert Marchetti in 1991 when he was working at Bill Marchetti's Latin, known as The Latin, and I was running Caffé e Cucina. To me, The Latin was the ultimate in Italian fine dining, and my business partners and I used to eat there whenever we could. Spending time there made us feel good; we never saw The Latin as competition, because we were all working towards the same goal of promoting Italian culture. We introduced to Caffé e Cucina the same principles of service that we saw at The Latin, but at a faster cafe pace.

Robert Marchetti

The development of Caffé e Cucina as an Italian identity brought a rapid growth within me. I felt that my role in the Italian community was growing. I felt that I could make a difference within, and for, the Italian community in Melbourne. I was also proud of the fact that I, and Caffé e Cucina, started to form an identity independent of Carlton, which had always been the traditional base of Italo-Australian culture in Melbourne.

As we grew more successful, some of our clients began to ask us to cater, to bring the spirit of Caffé e Cucina into their homes, so we created a catering company called La Panada. (*Panada* is the name given to a feast that originated in the Abruzzo region, at which people would eat for days, celebrating.) We had a great time, and we were very good at it, mainly because of the detail and effort we put into each and every occasion. I remember once spending six days setting up a function for 200 people: we polished every glass and piece of cutlery by hand. We always under-priced, over-catered and, not surprisingly, didn't make much of a profit. We were, however, very popular, and our clients were very happy with the work we did. After a while, we decided that we did not have the time or the resources to keep both the

Cartoon by Peter Nicholson celebrating Caffé e Cucina's fifth anniversary, 1993

'IT'S TINY, CRAMPED, CROWDED AND WE ABSOLUTELY LOVE IT. ANYONE WHO'S ANYONE . . . COMES HERE TO SIP THE BEST EXPRESSO IN TOWN, TO NIBBLE EXQUISITE ITALIAN PASTRIES AND EAT BODY-HUGGING CASALINGA COOKING.'

AUSTRALIAN GOURMET TRAVELLER, 1994

restaurant and the catering business functioning to the standard we wanted, so we closed La Panada and focused on Caffé e Cucina.

My son, Sylvester, was born in 1992, and this was also the year I went back to Italy for the first time in nearly seven years. It was wonderful to go back after having worked in the Australian food industry, and after the success of Caffé e Cucina I wanted to learn everything I could.

I spent a lot of time in Venice and I fell in love with the *bàcaro* style of wine bar. *Bàcaro* is a Venetian dialect word and is the name given to a tapas wine bar that serves little *ombretta* (a small glass of wine) and *pizzetti* (small tapas). The Venetians spend a lot of time in these little wine bars, and in the old days the locals would follow the shadow of the tower of the Basilica di San Marco in a *bàcaro* bar-hop. The more time I spent in these *bàcari*, the more I knew this was the perfect next step for me in Melbourne.

When I returned to Melbourne I started looking for a site for my new venture, Il Bàcaro. I wanted to be in the city. I wanted an element of discovery. I wanted my clients to feel like I felt when I wandered down the side streets of Venice and came across little *bàcari* and cafes. So, I ended up in Little Collins Street. Everyone said the area was dead, that no-one would go there, that it was a bad position, that it was dark and inhabited by unsavoury characters at night, but I knew it would be fantastic because it was mysterious and unexpected – exactly what I wanted for my *bàcaro*.

I had all the windows frosted and we kept the signage small so it would be a discovery for people. Il Bàcaro was very much a wine bar rather than a cafe. We started with breakfast, but not cooked breakfast; we served the pure Italian patisserie. All 60 wines on the list were available by the glass. Our whole approach was based on the Italian wine-bar philosophy.

Sylvester helps out at Caffé e Cucina, 1994

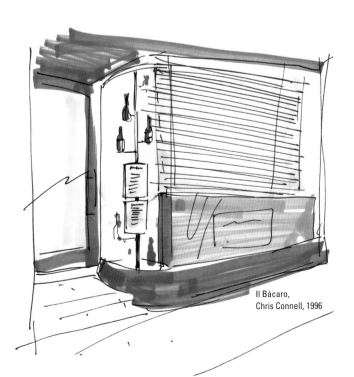

Il Bàcaro, Chris Connell, 1996

We were full from day one. It was very satisfying because Il Bàcaro really grew from Caffé e Cucina, and we, in turn, grew in the style of food we offered. Il Bàcaro's food, décor and atmosphere were well suited to Australia, to Melbourne. It was perfect.

In 1994 I helped create the first of what has become a popular kind of cafe – a car-gallery cafe. Dutton's, a prestige car gallery in Richmond, Melbourne, is housed in a very beautiful Art Deco building. The warehouse showroom is filled with prestigious old cars, and the walls are adorned with fine art. I helped set up Café Veloce, which brought together Italian food with fast, flashy cars. Dutton's has one of the best collections of Michelin memorabilia in the world – anyone who has a passion for car design visits Dutton's, and a lot of them eat at Café Veloce. The cafe is now in its tenth year of operation and is still very successful.

About six months after Il Bàcaro opened, I was approached about developing The George Hotel in St Kilda. The George has such a wonderful history and meant so much to me because I had spent a lot of my youth there. I had seen some of the great bands perform there: Hunters and Collectors, The Saints, The Models and The Birthday Party. I had a social connection with The George, as did many locals. I knew that Il Bàcaro was young enough for someone else to take over as the figurehead and, when I was offered the amazing opportunity to work with Donlevy Fitzpatrick at The George, I decided to move on. I left the Caffé e Cucina group but kept a small share. My leaving was a bit of a shock to everyone, particularly my father – he is still crying about it now.

So, in 1996 I said goodbye to Il Bàcaro and went off to put together The Melbourne Wine Room. Donlevy had been a huge influence on me, and I loved his philosophy: simplicity in all things. When it came to wine, he'd always say to me, 'I don't care if it's American oak or French oak, I just want to know whether it's good or bad.' This fitted exactly with my philosophy.

Café Veloce, 1994

We both thought that Karen Martini would be the perfect chef for The Melbourne Wine Room. At the time, she was working at the Kent Hotel in Carlton, and she was on a list we put together of accomplished, passionate people. She came in and cooked for us one day, and the list disappeared; we hired her on the spot. At that stage Karen was cooking very simple, modern Mediterranean and Italian food, creating flavours that were familiar to us – the first time my mother ate Karen's food, she told me it was food she would never cook but flavours she could recognise. Karen's style was perfect for The George, perfect for The Melbourne Wine Room. We had decided our menu would be more international than that at Caffé e Cucina.

While I was running The Melbourne Wine Room, I was also running a bar downstairs called The Snake Pit, which was incredibly successful. It played an interesting role in the development of Melbourne's bar culture because it was one of the few bars that were not clubs, not discos, but provided a similar environment in a bar atmosphere.

A lot of my Caffé e Cucina clients would not come down to The George because of the location and the types of people who loitered nearby. The area (Fitzroy Street, St Kilda) was still quite seedy at the time – we had to deal with prostitutes out the front and drug overdoses out the back. It challenged and confronted people, which is what I love. It didn't stop the crowds coming, though. The revamped George has been a great success.

My next passion became fast food, but not the type Australians usually associate with the term. I was interested in the way quick, cheap meals could be served to people on the run. At the time, you couldn't get good-quality fast food in Australia. After running The Melbourne Wine Room for four years, I went to Sydney and explored my ideas about fast food. I consulted with my friend Mario Venneri, who I had worked with at Caffé e Cucina, to create his cafe at Sydney airport, Cafe Italia. Mario drew inspiration

The Melbourne Wine Room, 1996

Karen Martini

Mahon&Band
graphics

from Caffé e Cucina when designing Cafe Italia, and he worked on the same philosophy of quality: why shouldn't you be able to get a good-quality meal just because you are in an airport?

Cafe Italia was, for five or six years in a row, voted among Sydney's top cafes, which was incredible considering it wasn't in a fashionable location. I loved my time at Cafe Italia because it gave me a break from Melbourne and allowed me to focus on fast food for a while.

People were surprised when I came back to Melbourne and, in association with my cousin Anthony, created Caffé Vini Spuntini in the Chadstone shopping centre. They were even more surprised when, after my professional success, I returned to working on the floor in a shopping centre. For me, the basis of Caffé Vini Spuntini was the same as for Cafe Italia: why not provide good-quality fast food in a shopping centre environment? Why should inner-city residents be the only ones exposed to quality?

When I started inspecting a new development at the wharf at Woolloomooloo a few months later in Sydney, a lot of people thought (once again) that I was crazy. They thought the location was terrible; no-one wanted to touch it. When I went to inspect the wharf, I thought it was a fantastic position. It was still a construction zone full of cranes and tractors and mess, but outside on the boardwalk it was tranquil and beautiful, I could see the whole city and the sun was shining. My idea for Otto Ristorante Italiano was to introduce a larger version of Caffé e Cucina to Sydney, maintaining the quality of product and service.

Otto (named because it was number eight at the wharf, and my eighth business venture) was a success from the beginning. Over the years, Caffé e Cucina and The Melbourne Wine Room had developed a loyal Sydney clientele, and that clientele came to Otto in force. The relationships I had built with my clients over the years were (and of course still are) very important to me, and, while we were now doing everything on a larger scale (Otto could seat 150 people, and it was the first time I had served food in

*Cafe Italia is a modern day miracle, a little piece of Italy that's been whisked up into thin air and plonked down in the international terminal at Sydney Airport. The coffee is so terrific, you almost wonder if you really should leave the country after all.*

Terry Durack

Chris Connell

that quantity), we still strove for the very best service that would allow our clients to step away from their everyday lives for a while.

Number nine – Nove Pizzeria – came about because we needed more room at Otto. We needed to expand our kitchen, and the tenancy next door hadn't been filled, but we couldn't take just part of the area . . . so, we took it all.

My whole concept for the wharf was to create a place where families could come and relax. If you went there on the weekend, there were kids everywhere, as well as couples, families and friends taking strolls. I wanted families to be able to come into Nove and have great pizza by the slice, like we used to have in Italy. We based everything around *nove* (nine): nine pizzas, nine pastas, nine white wines, nine red wines, nine ice-creams.

I loved Otto and Nove, and they really showed me how to move into big business. (When you start to order mineral water by the pallet rather than by the carton, things change.) While I was running these restaurants, I started looking at the possibility of doing something at the revamped Bondi Icebergs. For years I had visited Sydney and stayed with Mario Venneri in North Bondi, across the bay from the Icebergs, and each time we looked out at the Icebergs and said that it was the perfect location for a restaurant.

When the opportunity came up, I had to decide whether to maintain Otto and Nove, or put everything I had into Icebergs, and I chose the latter option. Icebergs Dining Room and Bar was my first real opportunity to create something that was completely Australian *and* international. To me, Icebergs is the pinnacle of everything I have ever done. It's a great beach house, and the experience you get when you walk through the door is one of relaxed dining by the water. Everything is very simple, and the menu is perfect for the location.

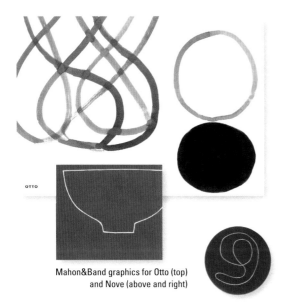

Mahon&Band graphics for Otto (top) and Nove (above and right)

Icebergs Dining Room and Bar, 2004

My restaurant layout and table design at Icebergs have come full circle from when I first set up Caffé e Cucina. I still use rectangular tables, and the spacing between tables is still very deliberate: just enough space between the tables for waiters and clients to move around, and wide enough apart to be private but not isolated. So, our clients become part of the restaurant. I love the sense of closeness and momentum this kind of dining creates; it's quite fascinating.

Icebergs is very much a long-term concept, and it has only just started. I was very lucky to have brought Karen Martini and Robert Marchetti with me to Sydney – their food is perfect for Icebergs; it is similar in character to what I have done before, but we have expanded our range. We have more Mediterranean flavours and a fuller menu, which suit our size and location. After two years with us at Icebergs Karen decided to return to Melbourne, but her influence will remain as Robert takes us into the future.

But, ultimately, my philosophy about food and service remains firm, and is the basis of the selection of recipes you will find as you read through this book: stick to simple, fresh ingredients and offer impeccable standards regardless of what type of experience you are offering.

Prepare and eat each meal as if it were your last.

Caffé e Cucina

Ricette

Colazione

To me, breakfast is fast, practical, simple and sweet. In Australia my parents adapted to a very Anglo-style breakfast based on cereals and cooked dishes. But in Italy I became fascinated with breakfast because it was fun and different to what I was used to. It was a social start to the day. Italy was obsessed with sweet breakfasts, and this passion has stayed with me. Breakfast became a coffee and a sweet pastry, and it is still a very simple part of my day.

In Pescara (in central Italy) we all lived in apartment blocks crammed on top of one another, so we all knew each other very well. Breakfast was part of that closeness. It was a chance to stop and catch up with friends at a bar on the way to school or work. Bar culture in Italy was an important part of breakfast, particularly in winter when it was cold and snowing — a cup of coffee or a hot chocolate was doubly welcome consumed in a cosy bar.

The recipes I have chosen for this **colazione** section are all dishes I enjoy for breakfast, and we loved serving this style of food at Caffé e Cucina. Here you will find a good selection from our menus over the years, and I have also included some of my mother's specialities. **Ciambella alla Gina** is one of my favourites. My family would often begin the day by sitting around and dipping the cake into bowls of milk or coffee. These recipes bring back great memories, and I want them to be fun.

# Bomboloni

## ITALIAN DOUGHNUTS

### Makes 20 small doughnuts

1 kg plain flour

40 g dry yeast

220 ml lukewarm water

200 g softened unsalted butter

2½ teaspoons salt

6 free-range eggs, beaten

50 g plain flour, extra

500 ml cottonseed oil

150 g caster sugar or vanilla sugar

Heap flour on a bench and make a well in the centre.

In a bowl, mix yeast and water, and stir until dissolved, then add to well in flour. Using your fingers, mix butter into flour, then mix in salt and beaten egg. Mix well to form a dough, then knead for 10–12 minutes, folding dough over and over. (To test dough, stretch it gently – it should slowly pull back into shape.)

Place dough in a clean bowl, then cover with a clean tea towel and set aside in a warm place and allow to prove (rise) for 2 hours, or until dough has doubled in size.

Transfer dough to bench, then gently knock dough back to its original size. Sprinkle extra flour over a board, then lay dough on board. Roll dough to the shape of a long sausage 5–6 cm thick and about 40 cm long.

Cut dough into small pieces (about the size of golf balls) and, with the palm of your hand, shape each piece into a ball. Lay balls on a lightly floured baking tray and set aside, uncovered, in a warm place for 20 minutes.

Heat oil in a large saucepan over medium heat. When oil reaches 176°C – to test, use a thermometer, or drop a piece of dough or stale bread into pan; if it sizzles immediately, the oil is ready (a thermometer is a better option because it will allow you to control the heat so the doughnuts cook evenly) – add one doughnut at a time. (Take care not to overcrowd the pan, and maintain oil temperature by keeping heat on medium.) Using a slotted spoon, gently turn doughnuts over to brown both sides. When doughnuts are golden brown, remove and place on kitchen paper while frying remaining doughnuts.

Sprinkle caster sugar on a clean tray and roll doughnuts through, coating all over. Serve doughnuts warm or cold with your favourite jam. The doughnuts will stay fresh for 5–6 hours.

*Cotechino alla griglia*

# Cotechino alla griglia

### GRILLED ITALIAN SAUSAGE

When I was growing up in Pescara, we would often go for a morning swim in summer and come home to my father cooking a mid-morning barbecue, which included *cotechino alla griglia*. I now enjoy this dish more as a hangover breakfast. It's great with a *sprizza* (see recipe on page 36).

Slice some thick pieces of cotechino (cured Italian pork sausage, available from butchers) and grill until crispy; sprinkle a little dried chilli over the cotechino as you turn them. Grill some of your favourite crusty bread, then either serve it all up on a plate or squash the cotechino together between two slices of the bread, and squeeze lemon over cotechino.

# Focaccia alla pugliese

### PUGLIESE-STYLE FOCACCIA

This focaccia originates in Puglia, in southern Italy. It's a great savoury breakfast, but it can be enjoyed all day, with many combinations – tomato, olives, anchovies, pine nuts – or a crispy late-night salad.

Serves 4–6

**6 large Desiree potatoes**

**2 tablespoons dry yeast**

**775 ml warm water**

**1 kg pizza flour
(or strong bakers' flour)**

**4 teaspoons sea salt**

**200 ml extra-virgin olive oil**

Preheat oven to hottest possible temperature.

Cut potatoes into quarters and place in a single layer on an oven tray. Bake for 20–30 minutes, or until soft. Mash warm potato until smooth. Whisk yeast through water. In the bowl of an electric mixer, combine flour and salt, then slowly mix in yeast mixture and potato. Mix on high for 10 minutes, then transfer dough to a clean bowl and set aside in a warm place to prove (rise) for 30–45 minutes, or until dough has doubled in size.

Spread dough to a 2 cm thickness on a baking tray and drizzle with oil. Bake for 25–30 minutes, or until cooked through and golden brown. Cut focaccia into desired sizes and serve with your favourite topping.

# Zabaglione al marsala

## BREAKFAST ZABAGLIONE

Serves 1

2 free-range egg yolks

50 g caster sugar

50 ml Marsala

This can also be served when you need a dessert in a hurry – just dust zabaglione with a little cocoa and serve with sponge finger biscuits.

### THE SUMMER VERSION

Place all ingredients in a bowl and whisk for 3–4 minutes, or until fluffy (the mixture should be thick and hold its form). Pour into a warm coffee cup and slug back.

### THE WINTER VERSION

Add 3–4 cm water to a saucepan and bring to a simmer. Place all ingredients in a bowl and hold bowl over simmering water (but do not let bowl touch water). Whisk for 3–4 minutes, or until fluffy (the mixture should be thick and hold its form) – do not allow mixture to become too hot. Pour into a warm coffee cup and slug back.

# Ricotta con miele

## RICOTTA WITH HONEY

Serves 1

200 g fresh ricotta

100 g vanilla (or plain) sugar

finely grated zest of ¼ lemon

100 ml chestnut (or plain) honey

30 g currants

30 g raisins

This is a classic breakfast that originated with Italian farmers, who have the pleasure of making their own ricotta. You can serve it on its own or with poached fruits such as rhubarb.

Preheat oven to 220°C.

Place ricotta in an ovenproof serving bowl. Sprinkle sugar and lemon zest over ricotta, and bake for 7–8 minutes. (Do not leave ricotta in oven too long, otherwise it will dissolve and collapse.) Remove from oven and drizzle honey over ricotta. Scatter currants and raisins on top and serve.

*Zabaglione al marsala*

# Focaccia ai fichi

## FIG FOCACCIA

**Serves 4**

**focaccia mix**

3½ teaspoons dry yeast

200 ml warm milk

200 ml warm water

500 g pizza flour
(or strong bakers' flour)

¾ teaspoon sea salt

50 ml olive oil

2 tablespoons olive oil, extra

**focaccia topping**

4 fresh figs

100 g fig jam (or any jam)

3½ teaspoons brown sugar

This is a Christmas breakfast – serve it with yoghurt, or with cream for dessert.

In a bowl, mix yeast with 100 ml warm milk and 100 ml warm water until yeast is completely dissolved, then set aside for 4 minutes until the mixture starts to bubble.

In a separate bowl, combine flour and salt. In a jug, combine yeast mixture, remaining milk and water, and oil. Mix well. Slowly pour wet mixture into dry ingredients, stirring with a wooden spoon to combine. When mixture thickens, remove spoon and begin mixing with your hands – checking for lumps – for 2 minutes. Lay dough on a clean, flat surface and knead with the palm of your hands for 5–6 minutes, or until smooth.

Pour half of the extra olive oil into a bowl and place dough on top. Pour the remaining oil over top of dough, and cover with a clean tea towel. (The oil will stop the dough from sticking to the bowl and tea towel.) Leave dough in a warm place to prove (rise) for 45–50 minutes, or until dough has doubled in size.

Transfer dough to bench and knead back to its original size. Roll dough to a rectangle 20 cm × 15 cm. Lay dough on a lightly oiled baking tray and leave in a warm place to prove (rise) for 25 minutes.

Preheat oven to 220°C.

Using a fork, prick dough, leaving 2–3 cm between each prick.

Slice figs into 1 cm discs.

Place fig jam and 1 teaspoon of cold water in a saucepan and melt over low heat. When jam has dissolved, remove from heat and allow to cool slightly.

With a pastry brush, paint melted jam over focaccia, leaving 2 cm clear around the edges. Scatter fig slices over jam (do not overlap them), then sprinkle sugar over the top. Bake for 14–18 minutes, or until focaccia begins to brown and crisp. Remove from oven and allow to cool for 5 minutes. Cut focaccia into desired sizes and serve warm.

# Pizzelle della Nonna

## NANNA'S PIZZELLE

A pizzelle is a traditional pizza biscuit. In Italy, *pizzelle della nonna* was a treat we only ever had on special occasions. We would sometimes have it with fig or grape marmalade, and always with a cappuccino. Centerba is an Italian digestive available from Italian delicatessens.

In a large bowl, combine eggs, sugar and sunflower oil, and mix well. Add centerba and lemon juice, then gradually sift in flour and mix to form a thick batter, ensuring there are no lumps. (The batter should coat the back of a metal or wooden spoon.) If batter is too thick, add a little water. If batter is too wet, blend a little flour with water and add to batter.

Heat olive oil in a heavy-based frying pan. Drop 1 tablespoon (per pizzelle) of batter into pan, taking care not to overcrowd the pan. Cook pizzelle until golden brown on both sides, then wrap in a clean tea towel to keep warm while you repeat process until all batter is cooked.

Choose your favourite marmalade and smear generously over pizzelle. Sandwich two pizzelle together and serve warm.

**Serves 4**

**8 free-range eggs**

**400 g caster sugar**

**400 ml sunflower oil**

**1 teaspoon centerba (optional)**

**juice of ½ lemon**

**400 g plain flour**

**10 tablespoons olive oil**

**your favourite marmalade**

figs

# Frittata

**100 ml olive oil**

**1 large Spanish onion, finely chopped**

**1 clove garlic, mashed**

**12 free-range eggs**

**200 g fresh parmesan, grated**

**sea salt and freshly ground black pepper**

**1 large ripe tomato, finely chopped**

**2 zucchini, finely grated**

**4 basil leaves, finely torn**

**½ bunch flat-leaf parsley, roughly chopped**

**olive oil, extra, for frying**

This frittata by Robert Marchetti can be enjoyed in many different ways – for breakfast, or late at night with a glass of wine and some fresh bread. Eggs are the king of this dish, so always use free-range eggs.

Preheat griller on low.

In a heavy frying pan, heat the 100 ml of olive oil. Add onion and garlic, lightly fry until transparent, then remove from heat and set aside to cool.

In a large bowl, whisk eggs with parmesan, and season with salt and pepper. Add tomato, zucchini, basil and parsley, and mix well. Add cooled onions and stir well. Check seasoning.

Wipe pan clean, coat with olive oil and return to heat. Pour in egg mixture and, with a wooden spoon, stir the slightly cooked egg mixture to centre of pan. Cease stirring. When mixture resembles runny scrambled eggs, remove from heat and place under griller. Grill until mixture is slightly firm but soft in the middle (like scrambled eggs), and lightly browned. Remove from under griller and place pan on a wire rack to cool.

When mixture has reached room temperature, shake pan using a backwards and forwards motion to release frittata from the sides. (Run a thin-bladed spatula underneath to ensure the frittata comes unstuck.) To remove frittata, place a large plate over the whole pan and flip over. Serve in wedges.

*Brioche alla cioccolata*

# Brioche alla cioccolata

## BRIOCHE WITH CHOCOLATE

This is one of my childhood addictions and a great energy starter. Some people might consider it a little simple and daggy, but you really must try it.

Preheat oven to 180°C.

Lay hazelnuts on a baking tray and bake for 6–8 minutes, or until golden and crunchy. Do not turn oven off but remove hazelnuts and roughly chop into bite-sized pieces.

Cut both pieces of brioche in half and place on a baking tray. Bake for 3–4 minutes, or until starting to brown. Remove from oven and transfer to a plate. Smear with butter (remember that brioche is butter-based) and generous lashings of Nutella, and sprinkle hazelnuts over top. Eat the brioche while they are hot.

Serves 2

**50 g fresh hazelnuts**

**2 × 250 g pieces brioche**

**50 g unsalted butter**

**100 g Nutella chocolate spread**

# Ciambella alla Gina

## GINA'S BREAKFAST CAKE

This book would not be complete without this recipe – coffee and my mother's ciambella have always been a part of my day. Do not be afraid to dip!

Preheat oven to 180°C.

Beat eggs and sugar until white and creamy. Add milk and lemon zest and mix well. Add flour, oil and yeast a little at a time, mixing well to remove lumps.

Pour mixture into a greased ciambella tin (if you do not have a ciambella – ring-shaped – tin, use a bread or baking tin) and bake for 35–40 minutes. To test the cake, insert a skewer in the centre; if it comes out clean, the cake is ready.

Serves 4

**4 free-range eggs**

**250 g caster sugar**

**300 ml milk**

**finely grated zest of 1 lemon**

**375 g plain flour**

**250 ml caster oil (or any plain oil)**

**6 teaspoons dry yeast**

# Panini al latte

## MILK BREAD ROLLS

**Makes 8–10 rolls**

550 ml milk

2 tablespoons fresh yeast

1 kg plain flour

3 teaspoons salt

50 g caster sugar

100 g powdered milk

200 g softened
unsalted butter

3 free-range eggs, beaten

3 extra free-range eggs,
beaten

This was a classic Caffé e Cucina breakfast. It was always a pleasure to arrive at work and smell these baking. Enjoy them plain or with leg ham and fontina cheese.

Warm 150 ml of the milk in a saucepan over low heat (or in a microwave); keep milk warm, not hot. Transfer milk to a bowl, add yeast and stir until dissolved. Add flour, remaining milk, salt, caster sugar, powdered milk, butter and beaten eggs, and mix with a wooden spoon for 10 minutes to form a dough. The dough should be elastic and durable. (To test dough, stretch it gently – it should slowly pull back into shape.)

Place dough in a clean bowl, then cover with a clean tea towel and set aside in a warm place to prove (rise) for 20 minutes, or until dough has doubled in size. Transfer dough to a bench, then gently knock dough back to its original size. Leave, uncovered, to prove for another 5 minutes.

Return dough to bench. Knead dough with the palm of your hand, pushing backwards and forwards and continually folding over, for 30 seconds.

Preheat oven to 200°C.

Lightly flour bench and roll dough into a sausage shape 6–7 cm thick and about 20–30 cm long. Cut dough into discs 3–4 cm thick, then mould into your preferred shape (such as round or long) and lay dough on a lightly oiled baking tray. Brush dough with the extra egg mix and bake for 5–8 minutes, or until golden brown and fluffy. (Don't leave panini in oven too long, otherwise they will dry out and crumble.) Serve warm.

Left to right: *caffè freddo, caffè speciale*

Left to right: *caffè sasà, macchiatone*

# Caffè

### caffè sasà  *Sasà's coffee*

We started making this coffee at Caffé e Cucina in 1989 for a special customer, Sasà. Sasà was a Neapolitan orthodontist who gave up his work to travel the world. He was staying in Melbourne for a while and we got to know him well. Sasà needed his sugar hit every morning, and that's what we gave him.

In an espresso cup, sprinkle a teaspoon of drinking chocolate over espresso coffee, then pour over a little warm milk, some more chocolate and a little milk again. Finish by sprinkling ground chocolate over the coffee.

**ground drinking chocolate**

**1 serve espresso**

**warm frothed milk**

**ground chocolate**

### caffè speciale  *espresso with cream and amaretto*

This has been with me since the birth of Caffé e Cucina. In an espresso cup, add amaretto, cream and espresso, then froth mixture until warm. Add sugar to taste.

**3 teaspoons amaretto**

**50 ml thickened cream**

**1 serve espresso**

**sugar, to taste**

### macchiatone  *my breakfast coffee*

This is my version of a half-latte. It is the perfect coffee for Australians because we love our coffee with milk. Sometimes too much milk can be heavy, so this is a good alternative.

You need one part espresso, one part warm milk and one part milk froth. Serve in a latte glass only half-full.

**espresso**

**warm frothed milk**

### caffè freddo  *my iced coffee*

This is wonderful. Add some cold milk (if desired) to sweeten espresso coffee, then pour over ice cubes in a cocktail shaker. Shake vigorously, then strain out ice cubes and serve.

**cold milk (optional)**

**sugar syrup or caster sugar, to taste**

**1 part espresso**

**ice cubes**

### rasentin  *a Venetian classic*

I only discovered this joy recently. Finish drinking your espresso as usual but don't use a spoon. Pour 2 teaspoons of Grappa in the empty, stained cup, then swirl and slug. What a heart-starter!

Aperitivo

**Aperitivo** is all about stimulating your appetite and preparing you for lunch or dinner. In Italy, **aperitivo** is an important, fun part of the day.

My father owned a cafe bar in Pescara, which was in the style of a traditional men's club–cafe. It was very old-school – there were hardly any women, and when I visited I had to take my earrings out before I walked in, and I wasn't allowed to wear black. My father served fantastic pastries for breakfast, and great coffee. Then, each day after breakfast had finished, he would set up for **aperitivo**. People would come into the bar at about eleven o'clock for a drink, some nuts, a chat and a cigarette. It was very ritualistic, very structured and very social. It allowed my father to run his bar and catch up with friends at the same time.

**Aperitivo** was not something that suited the Australian market when I first opened Caffé e Cucina, but the idea is gaining in popularity. Now, if you are entertaining at home, **aperitivo** is perfect. It's also great on weekends when you have friends over.

Campari, a traditional Italian drink, brings back warm memories for me because its consumption was a daily ritual in Italy. If you have a little Campari and some good company, what more do you need?

## Bicicletta

**45 ml Campari**

**100 ml dry white wine**

**ice cubes (if desired)**

Pour Campari and wine into a wine glass and mix. Finish with ice, if desired.

## Bittersweet

**¼ orange, peeled**

**45 ml Campari**

**30 ml pink grapefruit juice**

**crushed ice**

Place orange in bottom of a tall, wide-necked glass. Crush orange using a backwards and forwards motion with a spoon or pestle (this is called 'muddling'; it brings out the orange flavour). Pour in Campari and grapefruit juice, then top with crushed ice until glass is three-quarters full. Stir once more, then fill glass with more crushed ice.

## Campari and blood orange

**45 ml Campari**

**crushed ice**

**juice of a fresh blood orange**

In a highball (tall) glass, mix ingredients well. Enjoy. Blood oranges are only available between August and December. If you can't get blood oranges, the juice from an orange or ruby grapefruit will do the job just as well.

## Campari martini

**ice cubes**

**75 ml vodka**

**45 ml Campari**

**slice of orange**

Put ice in a large cocktail shaker, then pour in vodka and Campari. Stir, then strain mixture into your favourite martini glass. With a lighter, sear a portion of the orange slice and add to glass.

## Negroni

**crushed ice**

**wedge of orange**

**45 ml Campari**

**45 ml dry gin**

**1 tablespoon Cinzano Rosso**

Fill a large tumbler to the brim with ice and top with orange wedge. Pour in Campari, gin and Cinzano, and stir until mixed well.

## Negrita crush

**ice cubes**

**30 ml Bombay Sapphire gin**

**20 ml Cinzano Rosso**

**20 ml Campari**

**70 ml ruby red grapefruit juice**

**2 orange slices**

Fill 2 tall (highball) glasses to the rim with ice, then add (in the following order): gin, Cinzano, Campari and grapefruit juice. Drop in orange slices and 2 straws to serve.

## Number 8

**ice cubes**

**30 ml vodka**

**15 ml Campari**

**100 ml ruby grapefruit juice**

**wedge of lime**

Fill a short ('old-fashioned') glass with ice cubes. Pour in all remaining ingredients and mix well.

## Sprizza

**150 ml white pinot grigio**

**15 ml Campari**

**50–100 ml mineral water, to taste**

In a large (250 ml minimum) wine glass, add wine, then Campari. Add mineral water to taste, and serve.

# Bellini 1, 2, 3

These Bellini recipes are from Icebergs, which is a classic Mediterranean-influenced bar. These are great for a pre-meal drink or a lazy afternoon. For each Bellini recipe, use a chilled old-fashioned flat champagne glass – otherwise known as a Marie Antoinette glass.

## Bellini 1

**30 ml peach purée**

**120 ml Prosecco**

Pour peach purée into glass, add Prosecco and mix well. Serve.

## Bellini 2

**1 scoop watermelon sorbet or purée**

**5 ml rose water**

**120 ml Prosecco**

Place watermelon sorbet in glass, then pour rose water on top. Pour Prosecco over and agitate with a spoon to slightly mix sorbet.

## Bellini 3

**5 ml sugar syrup**

**10–12 basil leaves**

**20 ml strawberry purée**

**120 ml Prosecco**

In a shaker, add sugar syrup and basil. Agitate with a long spoon to release the basil flavour. Add strawberry purée and half the Prosecco, and stir well. Pour mixture through a strainer into glass. Pour remaining Prosecco over, and serve.

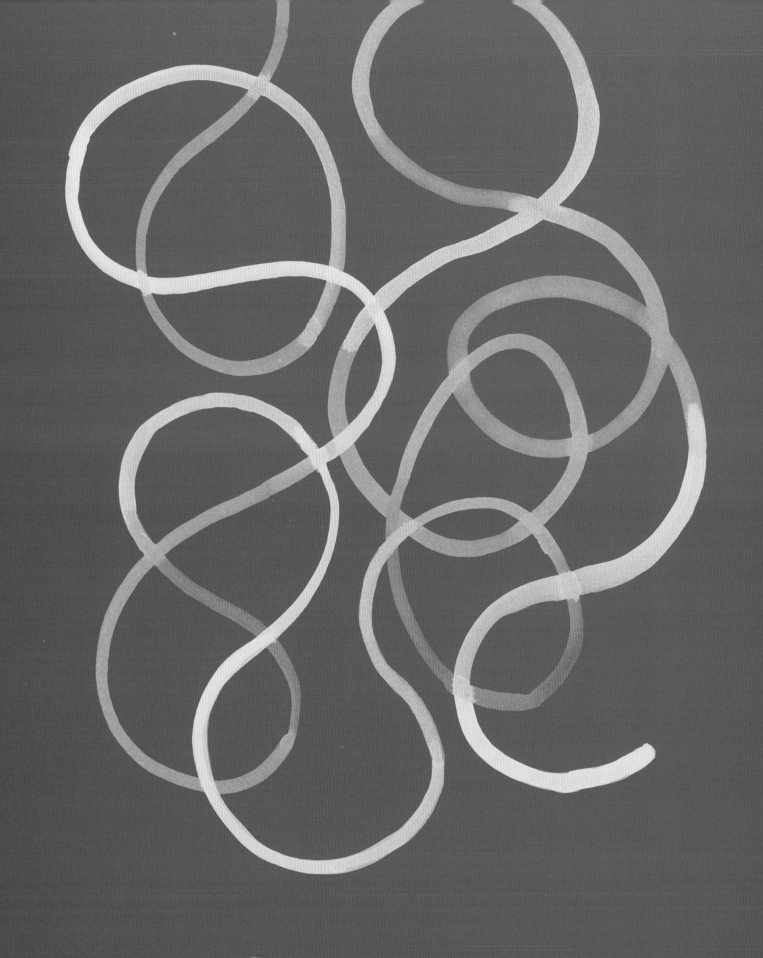

Pranzo

While I was growing up, lunch was the time we set aside to share a meal together as a family. Pasta always played a very important role. It's perfect: quick and easy, and the carbohydrates get you through the rest of the day. The classic meal to serve during an Italian summer is pasta with fresh tomatoes. I love the idea of crushing a tomato in your hand and throwing it into a pot of oil, then tossing in spaghetti, salt and fresh basil. In winter, you can use tomatoes to make a wonderful sauce.

Many of these **pranzo** dishes can be made as a **piatto di mezzo** (middle course) – sized between an entrée and a main – which is perfect for lunch.

None of the recipes require a lot of preparation. They are perfect for when you have friends drop in, and they can be cooked and served without fuss. When I cook, I always choose a recipe that takes me five minutes to prepare and ten minutes to cook. Basically, you cut it all up, you cook it and you eat it. For me, lunch is health- as well as taste-driven, so these meals are all quite light and nutritious.

This book is about what I want to cook for myself, regardless of whether or not I have friends over for a meal. These are not recipes that try to impress, they are recipes that make you feel good.

# Trofie pasta with kassler bacon, radicchio and ricotta

Serves 6–8

**500 g trofie pasta**

**220 ml olive oil**

**200 g kassler bacon, cut into 3 cm × 1 cm squares**

**5 eschalots, sliced**

**3 small red chillies, finely chopped**

**5 cloves garlic, finely chopped**

**sea salt and freshly ground black pepper**

**1 cup dry white wine**

**4 tablespoons chopped flat-leaf parsley**

**2 heads radicchio, washed and torn**

**250 g fresh ricotta, broken into chunks**

This is Karen Martini's twist on traditional carbonara. If trofie pasta is not available, use penne.

Bring a saucepan of salted water to the boil and add pasta. Cook until al dente, then drain and set aside.

Heat 100 ml of the olive oil in a large frying pan over medium heat and add bacon. Fry until brown, then add eschalots, chilli and garlic, and season with salt and pepper. Add wine and scrape pan to deglaze, then remove from heat.

Add pasta to pan and return to low heat. Stir mixture and add the remaining olive oil and parsley. Quickly stir in radicchio and cook for 1–2 minutes, or until slightly wilted. Add ricotta and stir gently, then add lots of pepper and serve immediately.

# Risotto con cozze in vino bianco

RISOTTO WITH MUSSELS IN WHITE WINE

Serves 4

2 litres chicken stock
(see recipe on page 180)

400 ml Riesling or Pinot Grigio

2 kg whole mussels in shells,
cleaned and debearded

100 ml extra-virgin olive oil

100 g unsalted butter

1 large onion, roughly
chopped

2 small red chillies,
deseeded and thinly sliced

4 cloves garlic, thinly sliced

2 bay leaves

500 g Arborio rice

sea salt and freshly ground
black pepper

½ bunch flat-leaf parsley,
roughly chopped

In a saucepan, bring chicken stock to the boil, then reduce heat and simmer.

Meanwhile, in a separate large saucepan, bring half the wine to the boil, then add mussels (taking care not to overcrowd the pan) and seal with a lid. Steam mussels for 5–6 minutes, or until they open. Strain mussels and set cooking liquid aside.

Remove mussels from shells, place mussels in a bowl and refrigerate immediately to stop the cooking process. Strain cooking liquid through a fine-mesh strainer and set aside.

In a heavy-based saucepan, heat oil and half the butter over low heat until butter has melted. Add onion, chilli, garlic and bay leaves, and cook for 3–4 minutes, or until soft (do not allow to brown). Add rice and stir gently until combined. Add half of the wine and simmer gently until liquid has evaporated. Season with salt and pepper (remember that mussels are already salty). Add a ladleful of hot chicken stock and simmer until liquid has evaporated. (Take care not to over-stir, otherwise the starch will break out of the rice and the mixture will become gluggy.) Repeat this process of adding stock and allowing it to evaporate for 25–35 minutes, or until rice is al dente.

Add remaining wine, chilled mussels and strained mussel liquid. Simmer for 5 minutes, or until mussels and rice are cooked. Remove from heat and mix in parsley and remaining butter, and check seasoning.

# Gnocchi con salsiccie e castagne

## GNOCCHI WITH SAUSAGES AND CHESTNUTS

**Serves 6**

**500 g chestnuts**

**80 g unsalted butter**

**6 pork sausages, sliced to around 1 cm thickness**

**2 Spanish onions, finely chopped**

**2 cloves garlic, thinly sliced**

**2 teaspoons dried chilli flakes**

**2 tablespoons finely chopped fresh sage leaves**

**150 ml red wine (anything light-bodied)**

**425 g can diced tomatoes**

**freshly grated nutmeg**

**sea salt and freshly ground black pepper**

**400 g gnocchi**

**grated fresh parmesan, to serve**

This is a great dish that Robert Marchetti discovered in a little Italian restaurant in Japan. He didn't think it was possible, but it was some of the best gnocchi he had ever eaten!

Bring a saucepan of water to the boil and add chestnuts. Boil for 45 minutes, or until semi-soft, then drain and set aside.

In a heavy-based frying pan, heat butter over medium heat until just brown, then add sausage. Fry until just brown, then add onion, garlic, chilli and sage and fry gently for 5 minutes, or until onions are soft. Increase heat to high and add wine. Cook, mixing well, until wine has evaporated. Decrease heat to low and add tomatoes, chestnuts and nutmeg to taste. Season with salt and pepper and simmer, stirring occasionally, for 30 minutes.

Bring a saucepan of salted water to the boil and add gnocchi. Cook until al dente, then remove from heat and drain. Mix through sauce and serve with parmesan.

chestnuts

# Agnolotti di ricotta al pomodoro
## AGNOLOTTI WITH RICOTTA AND TOMATO

This is my mother's traditional family recipe, which in Italy we would make for special celebrations. It's a little time-consuming but is worth the effort. Take care to use the best ricotta available.

Roll pasta dough to 2.5 mm thickness, then cut into 25 cm × 10 cm strips. Cover with a damp tea towel and set aside.

Place ricotta in a large bowl. Whisk 3 of the eggs and pour into ricotta. Season with salt, pepper and nutmeg, and mix well. Whisk remaining egg for brushing pasta dough, and set aside.

With a round pastry cutter, cut pasta into desired shapes (such as round or square). (If you do not have a pastry cutter, place a glass on the pasta and cut around the glass.) Lay a circle of pasta dough on your workbench and place a teaspoon of ricotta mix in the centre. Brush around edges with the whisked egg, then lay another pasta sheet on top and seal well, removing all air. Lay agnolotti on a floured tray. Repeat with remaining pasta, then refrigerate until needed.

Bring a large saucepan of salted water to the boil and add agnolotti. Cook until al dente.

Meanwhile, heat the *sugo di pomodoro in bottiglia* in a separate saucepan over low heat.

When agnolotti is ready, drain and serve under *sugo di pomodoro in bottiglia* with parmesan.

**Serves 4**

**1 quantity basic pasta dough (see recipe on page 168)**

**1 kg fresh ricotta**

**4 large free-range eggs**

**sea salt and freshly ground black pepper**

**freshly grated nutmeg**

**1⅔ cups *sugo di pomodoro in bottiglia* (see recipe on page 75)**

**grated fresh parmesan, to serve**

*Penne galbani*

# Sugo di pomodoro

TOMATO SAUCE

Every household should have this available as a staple.

In a large bowl, mash tomatoes with a potato masher, then add bay leaves and set aside.

Heat oil in a large saucepan over medium heat and add onion and garlic. Sauté for 3–4 minutes, or until the onion is soft and transparent. Add tomato and bay leaf mixture, then reduce heat and cook for 2 hours, stirring occasionally. Season with salt and pepper.

Makes 2.5 litres, with some left over to freeze.

**8 × 425 g cans peeled tomatoes**

**2 bay leaves**

**200 ml olive oil**

**6 onions, finely chopped**

**4 cloves garlic, finely chopped**

**sea salt and freshly ground black pepper**

# Penne galbani

PENNE WITH TALEGGIO AND ORANGE

This dish was inspired by a great staff meal we made at Caffé e Cucina. Use ribbed penne because it holds juices better than non-ribbed.

Bring a saucepan of salted water to the boil and add penne.

While penne is cooking, combine butter, parsley, Taleggio, orange juice and parmesan in a bowl and mix well. When pasta is almost al dente, remove from heat, drain and add to bowl. Season with salt and pepper and serve immediately.

Serves 2

**300 g ribbed penne**

**100 g softened unsalted butter**

**100 g flat-leaf parsley, roughly chopped**

**200 g Taleggio cheese, roughly chopped into 1 cm cubes**

**juice of 1 orange**

**200 g grated fresh parmesan**

**sea salt and freshly ground black pepper**

# Carpaccio di pesce spada con salvia fritta e capperi siciliano

## CARPACCIO OF SWORDFISH WITH FRIED SAGE AND SICILIAN CAPERS

**Serves 4**

**700 g whole fresh swordfish**

**juice of 2 lemons**

**200 ml extra-virgin olive oil**

**200 ml olive oil**

**16 fresh sage leaves**

**8 slices preserved lemon**

**sea salt and freshly ground black pepper**

**100 g salted capers (Sicilian are ideal)**

**2 lemons, cut into wedges**

The swordfish must be fresh; only buy from someone you trust. Good lemons and oil are the key to this dish; choose young, spicy extra-virgin olive oil.

With a sharp knife, slice fish as thinly as possible and lay out on a serving platter.

Place lemon juice in a bowl and slowly whisk in extra-virgin olive oil until emulsified (mixed well).

In a small, heavy-based frying pan, heat olive oil over high heat until hot (but not smoking). Add sage leaves and fry until crispy, then remove and place on absorbent paper to cool.

Dress fish with lemon juice mixture and preserved lemon and season with salt and pepper. Sprinkle sage leaves and capers over fish. Serve with lemon wedges and plenty of crusty bread.

# Fazzoletti di zucca

## BAKED PASTA WITH RICOTTA, SAGE AND PUMPKIN

Serves 4

600 g Japanese pumpkin, deseeded

100 ml olive oil

4 cloves garlic, finely chopped

1 bunch sage leaves, chopped

¼ teaspoon grated nutmeg

200 g grated fresh parmesan

2 free-range egg yolks

sea salt and freshly ground black pepper

1 quantity basic pasta dough (see recipe on page 168)

400 g ricotta

1 tablespoon olive oil, extra

1 bunch sage leaves, extra, picked

200 g shaved fresh parmesan

200 ml extra-virgin olive oil

This recipe may look long and difficult, but once you have tried it you will realise how easy it is. We served a version of this at Otto, and it is also great for a dinner party because you can prepare it a day ahead and bake it at the last minute.

Preheat oven to 160°C.

Cut pumpkin into medium-sized cubes, leaving skin on, and place on a baking tray. Bake for 50–60 minutes, or until pumpkin is soft and mushy. Remove from oven and allow to cool. With a spoon, scrape flesh from skin and place in a bowl. With a fork, lightly mash pumpkin until coarse, then set aside.

Heat olive oil in a frying pan over low heat and add garlic and chopped sage. Gently fry until soft, then remove and add to pumpkin mash. Add nutmeg, grated parmesan and egg yolks, and season with salt and pepper. Mix gently and set aside.

Lay a clean tea towel – 50 cm × 30 cm – on your workbench. With a pasta roller or rolling pin, and working on the bench beside the tea towel, roll pasta dough to 2.5 mm thickness, to the same dimensions as the tea towel. Lay pasta sheet over tea towel, then trim and discard any excess pasta that hangs outside its borders.

With a fork, smear ricotta to a 5 mm thickness over pasta sheet, leaving 1 cm clear around edges of the pasta sheet. Repeat process with pumpkin mixture, spreading it over the ricotta.

Begin rolling pasta (as you would a Swiss roll) from the 30 cm end, curling pasta inside itself until pasta is completely rolled. Use a little water to seal, pressing gently with your fingertips. Roll tea towel over pasta until firm and tight. Tie each end of tea towel with some cooking string until tight and sealed – you should now have something that resembles a large bonbon.

Half-fill a large, deep saucepan with well-salted water and place over low heat to simmer. Gently place pasta roll in water, ensuring it is covered with water (add more boiling water if necessary), and place a plate on top to keep it submerged. Simmer gently for 1¼ hours, then remove pasta roll from water, allow to cool and refrigerate until chilled.

Preheat oven to 220°C.

Heat a little olive oil in a frying pan over medium heat, then add picked sage leaves. Gently fry leaves until crisp, then remove and place on absorbent paper to drain.

Remove pasta roll from refrigerator. Untie string and remove tea towel. Slice pasta roll into discs 2–3 cm thick.

Lay pasta discs on a lightly oiled baking tray, then top with shaved parmesan. Bake for 12–15 minutes, or until cheese melts and starts to brown.

Arrange discs on plates, then sprinkle with fried sage leaves and drizzle with extra-virgin olive oil. The cooked pasta roll will keep, uncut and refrigerated, for 2–3 days.

Sage

# Linguine al pomodoro e ricotta

## LINGUINE WITH TOMATO AND RICOTTA

**Serves 6**

**1 quantity basic pasta dough (see recipe on page 168)**

**10 basil leaves**

**2 cups *sugo di pomodoro* (see recipe on page 47)**

**100 g grated fresh parmesan**

**300 g fresh ricotta, at room temperature**

**sea salt and freshly ground black pepper**

**extra-virgin olive oil, for drizzling**

This has been a favourite dish at Caffé e Cucina over the years – we served thousands – and it's a great, healthy lunch. A little goat's curd or stracchino cheese can be substituted for ricotta. You can use pre-packaged linguine if you don't have time to make your own.

(If you are using pre-packaged linguine, skip this paragraph and move to the next step.) Roll pasta dough to 2.5 mm thickness, then cut into 25 cm lengths. Run sheets through a pasta machine (or cut with a knife), then hang them on pasta rods (if you don't have pasta rods, use a broom handle balanced between two chairs) to dry for 3–4 hours, depending on the temperature in your kitchen. The linguine should still be agile.

Bring a saucepan of salted water to the boil and add linguine. Cook until al dente.

While pasta is cooking, add basil leaves to *sugo di pomodoro* and slowly heat in a heavy-based saucepan over low heat. When sauce is heated through, add parmesan, half the ricotta, salt and pepper to season, and a drizzle of extra-virgin olive oil.

When linguine is cooked, add to sauce. Sprinkle with small chunks of remaining ricotta to serve.

# Tagliolini con cozze e carciofi

## TAGLIOLINI WITH MUSSELS AND ARTICHOKES

**Serves 4**

**2 large fresh globe artichokes**

**200 ml dry white wine**

**2 kg whole mussels in shells, cleaned and debearded**

**500 g tagliolini pasta**

**200 ml olive oil**

**50 g butter**

**¼ bunch marjoram, chopped**

**4 cloves garlic, thinly sliced**

**2 small red chillies, thinly sliced**

**100 ml chicken stock (see recipe on page 180)**

**½ bunch flat-leaf parsley, roughly chopped**

**sea salt and freshly ground black pepper**

**extra-virgin olive oil, for drizzling**

I remember my mother making this dish when my father grew the first season of artichokes each year. If you can't find tagliolini pasta, use linguine.

Peel outer leaves from artichokes until you reach yellow, tender leaves. Trim 5 mm from top of artichokes and remove stalks. Slice artichokes thinly from top to bottom.

Add wine to a saucepan and bring to the boil. Add mussels (take care not to overcrowd the pan), seal with an airtight lid and steam for 5–6 minutes, or until mussels open. Remove from heat and strain, setting liquid aside.

Remove mussels from shells, place mussels in a bowl and refrigerate immediately to stop the cooking process.

Bring a saucepan of well-salted water to the boil and add tagliolini. Cook until almost al dente.

While pasta is cooking, heat olive oil and butter in a frying pan over high heat. When butter has melted, add artichokes, marjoram, garlic and chilli and fry gently (do not allow to brown) for 5–6 minutes, or until artichokes are tender. Reduce heat to low, add stock and reserved mussel juice and simmer for 2–3 minutes. Add mussels and parsley, then add tagliolini and season with salt and pepper. Cook over a low heat for 1–2 minutes, allowing pasta to absorb all the flavours. Remove from heat and finish with a drizzle of extra-virgin olive oil.

parsley

# Spaghetti con sugo di carne

## SPAGHETTI WITH A MEAT SAUCE

This pasta is from Abruzzo, and was my Aunt Mena's speciality. She would cook this for us on family occasions. When my mother makes this dish, she always adds a little chilli (dried is best) at the end to wake my spirit (or possibly punish me).

Roll pasta dough to 4 mm thickness, then cut into 25 cm lengths. Run sheets through a pasta machine (or cut with a knife), then hang them on rods (if you don't have pasta rods, use a broom handle balanced between two chairs) to dry for 1–2 hours, depending on the temperature in your kitchen. The spaghetti should still be agile.

In a large, heavy-based saucepan, heat oil and half the butter over medium heat. Add pancetta, onion, leek, carrot, celery and bay leaves, then fry gently until vegetables are soft. Add pork, veal, sausage, chicken liver and garlic, then increase heat to high and fry until meat is golden brown. Add wine and tomato paste, and season with salt and pepper. Bring to the boil, then reduce heat and simmer for approximately 1 hour, or until thickened.

Add tomatoes and continue to simmer for 30–40 minutes. (The slower you cook the sauce, the more developed the flavour will be.)

Meanwhile, bring a saucepan of salted water to the boil and add spaghetti. Cook until 2 minutes from al dente, then drain. Return spaghetti to pan, then add meat sauce and parsley. Season with salt and pepper and reduce heat to low. Stir well until pasta is al dente. (Do not over-stir, otherwise the spaghetti will begin to break.) If the sauce seems a little dry, add some of the pasta water to bring the sauce back to life. Drizzle with extra-virgin olive oil and serve with parmesan.

Serves 4

1 quantity basic pasta dough (see recipe on page 168)

200 ml olive oil

100 g unsalted butter, roughly chopped

200 g pancetta, finely chopped

2.5 brown onions, finely chopped

4 leeks, finely chopped

2 large carrots, finely chopped

2 sticks celery, finely chopped

3 fresh bay leaves (or 2 dried)

400 g coarsely minced pork

400 g coarsely minced veal

300 g cured coarse pork sausage, finely chopped

200 g chicken livers, finely chopped

4 cloves garlic, finely chopped

150 ml dry white wine

50 g tomato paste

sea salt and freshly ground black pepper

10 ripe tomatoes, finely chopped

250 g tinned chopped tomatoes

½ bunch flat-leaf parsley, roughly chopped

sea salt and freshly ground black pepper

50 ml extra-virgin olive oil

300 g grated fresh parmesan

# Orecchiette con broccoli e cavolfiore

## ORECCHIETTE WITH BROCCOLI AND CAULIFLOWER

**Serves 4**

**600 g broccoli, roughly chopped**

**200 g cauliflower, roughly chopped**

**100 ml olive oil**

**2 large cloves garlic, thinly sliced**

**2 small red chillies, finely chopped**

**8–10 large anchovy fillets in oil**

**½ bunch flat-leaf parsley, chopped**

**sea salt and freshly ground black pepper**

**500 g orecchiette pasta**

**100 g grated fresh parmesan**

**50 ml extra-virgin olive oil**

In this dish, Karen Martini has managed to capture the flavours of the Mediterranean and the tastes of a southern Italian summer.

Bring a saucepan of water to the boil and add broccoli. Cook for 6–8 minutes, or until tender. Drain, setting aside 150 ml of the cooking liquid.

Add fresh water to the pan and bring to the boil. Add cauliflower and cook for 8 minutes, or until tender, then drain and squeeze out excess water. Set aside.

In a large frying pan, heat olive oil over medium heat, then add garlic, chilli and anchovies. Cook, breaking up and mashing anchovies as they heat, but do not allow garlic to brown. Add broccoli and mash well with the back of a spoon. When broccoli has heated through, add cauliflower, half the parsley and the reserved cooking liquid. Bring mixture to the boil and season with salt and pepper. Remove pan from heat and set aside.

Bring a saucepan of salted water to the boil and add orecchiette. Cook until al dente, then drain.

Return sauce to heat and toss in pasta. Heat through and stir in parmesan and remaining parsley. (Add a little water if the sauce is too thick.) Spoon into large, heated pasta bowls, then drizzle with extra-virgin olive oil to serve.

# Insalata di frutti di mare

## SEAFOOD SALAD

This is a summer night's salad and is great with crusty bread to mop up the juices. Ask your fishmonger to prepare the seafood for you.

In a heavy-based saucepan, heat 100 ml of the olive oil over medium heat. Add mussels, clams and wine, then seal with a lid and steam for 4–5 minutes, or until mussels and clams open. Remove and strain, retaining broth. Set broth and clams aside separately (leave clams in their shells). Check mussels for any remaining beards and remove mussels from their shells. Discard shells and set mussels aside.

Clean the pan, then heat the remaining olive oil over medium heat. When hot, add scampi, prawns, garlic, chilli, fennel and capers, and season with salt and pepper. Fry gently for 3 minutes, then add scallops, calamari and tomato, and fry for 1 minute. Add chicken stock and reserved mussel broth and simmer for 3–4 minutes, or until prawns are cooked. Remove pan from heat and add crabmeat, mussels, clams, lemon juice, chives and parsley. Mix well and check seasoning. Drizzle with extra-virgin olive oil and serve.

Serves 4

**200 ml olive oil**

**10 whole mussels in shells, cleaned and debearded**

**10 fresh clams in shells**

**100 ml white wine**

**4 scampi, halved and deveined**

**12 medium-sized green prawns, shelled and de-veined**

**4 garlic cloves, sliced**

**2 small red chillies, finely chopped**

**1 small head young fennel tops, finely chopped**

**50 g salted baby capers (Sicilian are ideal), washed**

**sea salt and freshly ground black pepper**

**10 scallops, shelled**

**200 g fresh calamari, sliced in rings**

**2 ripe tomatoes, thinly sliced**

**200 ml chicken stock (see recipe on page 180)**

**100 g cooked crabmeat**

**juice of 1 lemon**

**1 bunch chives, finely chopped**

**½ bunch flat-leaf parsley, finely chopped**

**100 ml extra-virgin olive oil**

# Risotto con porcini e Grana

## RISOTTO WITH PORCINI MUSHROOMS
## AND GRANA CHEESE

**Serves 4**

**2 litres chicken stock
(see recipe on page 180)**

**200 g dried porcini
mushrooms, cut into
bite-sized pieces**

**150 g unsalted butter**

**200 ml olive oil**

**400 g fresh shiitake
mushrooms, cut into
bite-sized pieces**

**200 g field mushrooms,
cut into bite-sized pieces**

**½ bunch picked thyme leaves**

**1 large onion, roughly
chopped**

**4 cloves garlic, thinly sliced**

**2 bay leaves**

**500 g Arborio rice**

**100 ml dry white wine**

**sea salt and freshly ground
black pepper**

**300 g grated Grana Padama
(or fresh parmesan)**

**½ bunch flat-leaf parsley,
roughly chopped**

This is a bestseller in most Italian restaurants in the country; a great classic.

In a saucepan, bring chicken stock and porcini mushrooms to the boil, then reduce heat to simmer.

Meanwhile, in a heavy-based frying pan, heat 50 g of the butter and half the oil over low heat until butter has melted. Add shiitake mushrooms, field mushrooms and thyme and gently fry for 5–6 minutes, or until mushrooms are soft. Remove from heat and set aside.

In a separate, heavy-based frying pan, heat 50 g of the butter and the remaining oil over low heat until butter has melted. Add onion, garlic and bay leaves and cook for 3–4 minutes, or until onion is soft (do not allow to brown). Add rice and stir gently until combined. Add wine and simmer gently until liquid has evaporated. Season with salt and pepper (remember that porcini mushrooms are salty). Add a ladleful of hot chicken stock and simmer until liquid has evaporated. (Take care not to over-stir, otherwise the starch will break out of the rice and the mixture will become gluggy.) Repeat this process of adding stock and allowing it to evaporate for 25–35 minutes, or until rice is al dente.

Add mushrooms and simmer for 5 minutes, or until rice is cooked. Remove from heat and gently stir in Grana Padama, parsley and remaining butter.

# Pasta e fagioli

## PASTA WITH BEANS

This dish is a reminder that food and tradition work very well together. This is a recipe of my mother's, and we grew up with it in Italy. It is heaven during winter. You need to plan in advance for this one, because you must soak the beans overnight.

Rinse beans in plenty of cold water. Bring a saucepan of salted water to the boil and add beans. Cook for 25–30 minutes, or until just tender, then remove from heat and set aside in cooking liquid.

Heat oil in a heavy-based frying pan. Add sausage and onion and fry until golden brown. Add wine and cook until wine has evaporated. Reduce heat and add tomato purée, and season with salt and pepper. Simmer for 10 minutes, or until sauce is thick. Add drained beans and simmer for 10 minutes. Keep pan over heat while moving to next step.

Bring a saucepan of well-salted water to the boil. Meanwhile, roll pasta dough to sheets about 5 mm thick. Cut dough roughly into 1 cm × 4 cm strips. Add pasta to boiling water and cook until almost al dente. Remove pasta and drain, then add to warm bean mixture. Simmer for 2–3 minutes until pasta is al dente.

Check seasoning and serve with dried chilli and parmesan.

**Serves 4**

**1 kg dry borlotti beans, soaked overnight in cold water**

**100 ml olive oil**

**400 g cured pork sausage, finely chopped**

**¼ brown onion, finely chopped**

**250 ml dry white wine**

**2 × 425 g cans tomato purée**

**sea salt and freshly ground black pepper**

**1 quantity basic pasta dough (see recipe on page 168)**

**1 teaspoon dried chilli flakes**

**200 g grated fresh parmesan**

# Maltagliata di manzo

## ROUGH-CUT STEAK

*Maltagliata di manzo* is a fantastic *piatto di mezzo* (middle dish) and it is perfect for when you are cooking just for yourself. This dish came to represent the philosophy behind Caffé e Cucina: simple flavour, great texture, no fuss. This dish is also fast to make at home – while we were building Icebergs at Bondi, Sydney, it was quicker for me to go home and make this dish than to go out and buy something for lunch. Just throw all the ingredients into a dish and dress it with a bit of olive oil, a wedge of lemon and some rocket; or try it with ricotta, goat's cheese or capsicum. It's open to all sorts of interpretations.

Arrange rocket in a large serving bowl and drizzle with extra-virgin olive oil and a squeeze of lemon. Set aside.

In a separate bowl, season flour with salt and pepper. Slice beef into thin strips (cut against the grain to retain tenderness) and lightly coat with the seasoned flour. Heat a heavy-based frying pan over high heat and add olive oil. Add beef and fry until golden brown but still moist. (Take care not to stir the beef too much, because stirring will release the juices and the beef will begin to stew rather than fry.) When meat is almost ready, add balsamic vinegar (this will caramelise the juices from the pan), then remove beef and juices. Add beef strips to rocket salad and serve with a wedge of lemon.

Serves 1

**150 g rocket**

**100 ml extra-virgin olive oil**

**½ lemon**

**100 g plain flour**

**sea salt and freshly ground black pepper**

**200 g porterhouse steak**

**100 ml olive oil**

**50 ml balsamic vinegar**

**1 lemon, halved**

# Quadretti e piselli

## PASTA WITH PEAS

Serves 4

**6 very ripe tomatoes**

**2 large free-range eggs**

**salt**

**250 g pizza flour
(or strong bakers' flour)**

**1 teaspoon olive oil**

**100 ml olive oil, extra,
for cooking**

**1 kg fresh peas, shelled
(you can use frozen peas)**

**¼ brown onion, finely chopped**

**freshly ground black pepper**

**¼ bunch flat-leaf parsley,
roughly chopped**

**6 basil leaves, torn**

**200 g grated fresh parmesan**

**1 teaspoon dried
chilli flakes (optional)**

This is my all-time favourite soup. My mother used to make this regularly, and the taste will stay with me always.

Place tomatoes in the bowl of an electric mixer. Purée and set aside.

In a bowl, beat both eggs with a pinch of salt.

Heap flour on a bench and make a well in the centre. With a fork, slowly mix in beaten eggs, then add the teaspoon of oil to form a smooth dough. Roll dough to around 5 mm thickness. With a sharp knife, cut dough into small squares about the size of the peas.

Place a frying pan over medium heat and add oil. When oil is warm (not hot), add peas and onion, and season with salt and pepper. Sauté gently for 3–5 minutes, or until peas are tender, then add parsley, basil and the puréed tomato. Reduce heat and simmer for 15–20 minutes, or until sauce has thickened and acid has been removed from tomatoes (to check acid, taste the mix). (Don't worry if the peas turn slightly brown – the taste is the most important thing.)

Meanwhile, bring a saucepan of salted water to the boil. Add pasta and cook for 3 minutes, or until pasta is al dente. Drain pasta but keep 200–300 ml of the cooking liquid.

Add pasta to pea sauce. Check seasoning, and if sauce is a little dry, add reserved cooking liquid. Serve with parmesan and dried chilli to taste.

# Pappardelle con spugnole e asparagi

## PAPPARDELLE WITH MORELS AND ASPARAGUS

In 1997 Karen Martini introduced me to morels, freshly picked by a gypsy woman in the Victorian Grampians. This dish she created makes a wonderful lunch. Morels are only available for 3–4 weeks of the year (in October and November), so be on the lookout and make this dish a special occasion.

Bring a large saucepan of salted water to the boil and add pappardelle. Cook until almost al dente, then add asparagus and cook until pappardelle is al dente (about 2 minutes). Drain.

In a heavy-based frying pan, melt butter over medium heat. Add morels and garlic, and sauté for 2 minutes. Add half the chicken stock and simmer gently for 6–8 minutes, or until sauce begins to thicken. Add truffle paste and scrape around the pan to deglaze. Add pappardelle, asparagus and remaining stock, then mix well and heat through.

To serve, sprinkle with parmesan, chives and a squeeze of lemon.

Serves 4

**400 g dried pappardelle pasta**

**16 spears asparagus, peeled and cut into long slivers**

**200 g unsalted butter**

**300 g fresh morel mushrooms**

**3 cloves garlic, thinly sliced**

**400 ml chicken stock (see recipe on page 180)**

**3 tablespoons black truffle paste**

**100 g grated fresh parmesan**

**½ bunch chopped chives**

**½ lemon**

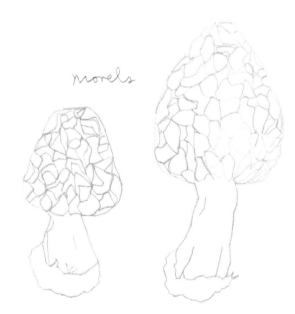

morels

# Calamari St Andrea

### FRIED CALAMARI

**Serves 4**

1 kg small-to-medium fresh
calamari, cleaned (you can buy
the calamari already cleaned)

200 g plain flour

sea salt and freshly ground
black pepper

150 ml extra-virgin olive oil

juice of 4 lemons

4 handfuls rocket

1 litre olive oil, for frying

200 g balsamic mayonnaise
(see recipe on page 168) or
tartare sauce

2 lemons, cut into wedges

This has been a Caffé e Cucina favourite, and we became famous
for it. It used to be something the staff cooked for ourselves, but
then one day a customer saw it and asked for it, and it all went from
there. It is the perfect *piatto di mezzo* – just the right size for lunch.
Fresh calamari is essential to the success of this recipe – if you can't
get fresh, you may as well cook a bowl of pasta instead!

Slice calamari into thin strips approximately 6 cm long and 6–8 mm thick.
Season flour generously with salt and pepper, then lightly dust calamari with it.
Shake calamari to remove excess flour.

In a bowl, combine extra-virgin olive oil and lemon juice, and season with salt
and pepper. Mix well and set aside.

In a deep, heavy-based saucepan, heat olive oil to around 200°C – to test, use
a thermometer or fry a little of the calamari or a piece of stale bread; it should
sizzle as soon as you drop it in the oil. Add calamari in batches, making sure
not to overcrowd the pan, and cook each batch for 2–3 minutes, then drain on
absorbent paper. Check seasoning and keep calamari warm on a tray in the
oven while cooking remaining batches.

Add rocket to lemon juice mix. Combine, then arrange on a serving plate.
Arrange calamari on rocket and add a dollop of balsamic mayonnaise or tartare
sauce and lemon wedges on the side. Serve immediately.

# Pacheroni al forno con peperoni brasati e Taleggio

BAKED PASTA WITH BRAISED PEPPERS AND TALEGGIO

Serves 4

500 g pacheroni pasta

200 ml olive oil

4 large red capsicums, sliced into 1 cm-thick strips

4 cloves garlic, thinly sliced

2 small red chillies, thinly sliced

½ bunch flat-leaf parsley, finely chopped

200 g Taleggio cheese, roughly chopped

300 g grated fresh parmesan

sea salt and freshly ground black pepper

200 ml extra-virgin olive oil

If pacheroni pasta is not available, use large penne or rigatoni.

Preheat oven to 240°C.

Bring a saucepan of salted water to the boil and add pacheroni. Cook until al dente, then drain and set aside.

Heat olive oil in a heavy-based frying pan over high heat, then add capsicum, garlic and chilli. Fry until capsicum is brown and soft, then remove from heat and set aside to cool.

In a bowl, combine pasta, capsicum mix, parsley, Taleggio and a third of the parmesan. Season with salt and pepper and drizzle with extra-virgin olive oil.

Transfer pasta to a heavy-based baking dish and sprinkle remaining parmesan over the top. Bake for 15–20 minutes, or until brown.

# Spaghetti alla puttanesca

SPAGHETTI WITH A SAUCE OF TOMATO AND OLIVE

Serves 4

olive oil, for cooking

½ clove garlic, chopped

1 brown onion, finely chopped

½ bunch oregano, chopped

2 bay leaves

3 cups white wine

1 litre *sugo di pomodoro* (see recipe on page 47)

sea salt and freshly ground black pepper

500 g spaghetti

grated fresh parmesan, to serve

This wonderful pasta dish has been unduly criticised because it has been made (badly) for years. When made well, it is delicious.

Pour enough oil to cover the base of a large, heavy-based frying pan. Combine garlic, onion, oregano, bay leaves, wine and *sugo di pomodoro* in pan and cook slowly over low heat for 1 hour, stirring occasionally. Season with salt and pepper.

Bring a saucepan of salted water to the boil and add spaghetti. Cook until al dente, then drain and add to sauce. Stir to combine, then serve with parmesan.

# Rigatoni con asparagi

## RIGATONI WITH ASPARAGUS

This is Robert Marchetti's version of a summer carbonara. I have enjoyed this over many late-night conversations – thank you, Robert. Guanciale (cured pork cheek) is available from Italian delicatessens; if Guanciale is not available, use pancetta (Italian bacon). Guanciale will keep in your refrigerator for up to 6 weeks.

Bring a saucepan of well-salted water to the boil.

Trim asparagus spears to 3 cm and set aside. Add stalks to boiling water and cook for 2–3 minutes, or until tender. Remove asparagus stalks and discard. (The asparagus has now flavoured the water.) Add rigatoni to water and cook until al dente, then drain.

In a cold frying pan (a cold pan allows you to increase heat slowly and avoid burning the ingredients), combine oil, butter, lemon thyme, garlic, asparagus spears and Guanciale and fry gently over medium heat for 4–5 minutes, or until Guanciale is crispy and asparagus is tender. Reduce heat to low and add cream and parmesan, and season with lots of pepper and a little salt (remember that Gaunciale and parmesan are salty). Simmer gently for 2 minutes, then add rigatoni and lemon juice to pan, mix well and check seasoning before serving.

**Serves 4**

**500 g asparagus**

**400 g rigatoni**

**50 ml olive oil**

**50 g unsalted butter**

**½ bunch picked lemon thyme leaves**

**4 cloves garlic, thinly sliced**

**200 g Guanciale, thinly sliced**

**200 ml thickened cream**

**200 g grated fresh parmesan**

**sea salt and freshly ground black pepper**

**juice of ½ lemon**

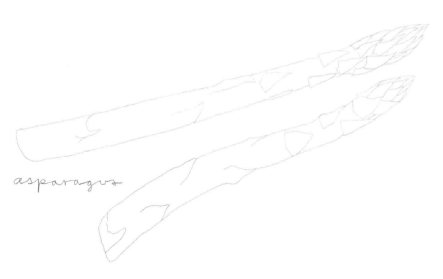

asparagus

# Squazzata di cozze

## MUSSELS IN TOMATO BROTH

Serves 4

150 ml olive oil

2 kg whole mussels in shells,
cleaned and debearded

4 cloves garlic, thinly sliced

2 small red chillies,
finely chopped

200 ml dry white wine

1 cup flat-leaf parsley,
roughly chopped

400 ml *sugo di pomodoro*
(see recipe on page 47)

4 thick slices sourdough bread

*Squazzata di cozze* is a wonderful meal to share and is one of my all-time favourites. This dish has been on almost every menu I have been involved with, from Caffé e Cucina to Otto and Nove and now Icebergs. The key to this dish is the also key to my whole philosophy of dining: quality and simplicity.

In a heavy-based saucepan, heat oil and add mussels, garlic and chilli. Stir for 2 minutes, or until mussels begin to open, then add wine and parsley, tomato, seal pan with an airtight lid and cook for 2–3 minutes, or until mussels open fully. Discard any closed mussels.

Meanwhile, toast sourdough bread until crunchy and dry.

When mussels have opened, serve with toasted bread.

*Spaghetti con vongole e zucchini*

# Spaghetti con vongole e zucchini

## SPAGHETTI WITH CLAMS AND ZUCCHINI

Bring a saucepan of salted water to the boil and add spaghetti. Cook until almost al dente.

While spaghetti is cooking, heat oil in a heavy-based saucepan over high heat and add clams, garlic and chilli. Stir for 1 minute, then add wine, seal with a lid and cook for 4 minutes. Add zucchini and cook for a further 1–3 minutes, or until clams have opened. Discard any closed clams.

Strain spaghetti and add to clams. Stir through parsley and lemon juice and season with salt and pepper to finish. The sauce will be quite brothy – don't worry, that's what a piece of crusty bread is for!

**Serves 4**

**500 g spaghetti**

**200 ml olive oil**

**1 kg fresh clams in shells**

**6 cloves garlic, thinly sliced**

**2 small red chillies, deseeded and thinly sliced**

**200 ml white wine**

**6 baby zucchini, shaved**

**½ bunch flat-leaf parsley, roughly chopped**

**juice of 1 lemon**

**sea salt and freshly ground black pepper**

# Penne con rucola

## PENNE WITH ROCKET

This is a great 'nothing in the fridge' late-night meal, particularly in summer.

Bring a saucepan of salted water to the boil and add penne. Cook until al dente, then drain and set aside.

Heat oil in a frying pan over low heat. Add garlic and chilli and cook until both begin to brown. Add rocket and cook for 20 seconds, until just wilted. Add penne, then season with salt and pepper, squeeze over lemon juice and finish with parmesan.

**Serves 2**

**250 g penne**

**150 ml olive oil**

**2 cloves garlic, thinly sliced**

**1 small red chilli, deseeded and thinly sliced**

**handful rocket**

**sea salt and freshly ground black pepper**

**juice of 1 lemon**

**150 g grated fresh parmesan**

# Sugo di pomodoro in bottiglia

## BOTTLED TOMATO SAUCE

While I was growing up in Pescara, this sauce was a big part of my life. Every family should have a bottle for each week of the year. This recipe makes 3 cups, and if you keep it in a cool, dark place, this sauce will last for 3–4 years. You will need a few pieces of equipment, including something heavy such as an olive-oil tin, a funnel, a few old tea towels, a sterilised empty bottle with a lid (if possible, use a new, unused bottle without residue) and a large pan to hold the bottle.

Wash tomatoes in warm water to remove any soil or impurities. Slice tomatoes in half and squeeze out seeds (a few left in won't hurt). Lay tomatoes in a colander or strainer with a heavy weight on them to squeeze out all remaining water. Purée tomatoes in a blender to your preferred chunkiness (if you don't have a blender, push tomatoes through a sieve).

Place a funnel in the opening of your bottle and pour sauce into the bottle. Secure the lid, pressing to ensure a tight seal. Place bottle in a large, deep saucepan and cover completely with cold water. Slowly bring to the boil, then reduce heat and simmer for 1 hour. Allow to cool in the water.

To add extra flavour to your sauce, add a little fresh basil before bottling.

**Makes 3 cups**
(enough to fill a standard wine bottle or a large beer bottle)

**6 very ripe Roma tomatoes**

Spuntino

*Spuntino* is a fun part of the day. In Italy, whether it was summer or winter, **spuntino** was a snack we would have between three and five o'clock in the afternoon to tide us over until dinner. *Spuntino* would be a slice of pizza, or an Italian baguette, or ciabatta with olive oil and tomatoes from the garden. It doesn't need to be any fancier than a piece of bread and a squashed tomato.

The best part about the recipes in this chapter is that they are guides. So, have some fun with the ingredients. The key to the dishes here is not the preparation — that's the easy part — but in purchasing the product. Make sure you buy everything fresh. We always bought mozzarella fresh each day. We always bought good tomatoes, and we always had prosciutto. It's so easy to throw it all together in a roll.

In Australia, the afternoon snack is becoming more popular, because, I think, we are eating later in the evening. These **spuntino** dishes are great for kids, particularly if you have spent the day at the beach and come home a bit hungry but you don't really want to have lunch. They're also great if someone pops in unexpectedly.

At Caffé Vini Spuntini in Melbourne, we served pizza by the slice, which is a very Roman thing. A lot of people also stopped into Caffé e Cucina on the way to somewhere else, and our afternoon snacks and coffees were very popular. Snack time can be a great social time, and **spuntino** dishes are the perfect size to share. Now, at Icebergs at Bondi, we are finding that Saturday and Sunday afternoons are becoming a very popular time to come in for a glass of wine and a snack. But with these dishes, you can enjoy the same experience at home.

# Panini

ITALIAN ROLLS

Panini are eaten in every part of Italy. There are hundreds of ways to fill them; here are my favourite four. No fuss, no experimentation – just the classics.

### PANINI SAN DANIELE

*Roll filled with prosciutto, rocket and parmesan*

Split the bread roll in half and brush with a little extra-virgin olive oil. Add paper-thin slices of prosciutto cut fresh from your deli, then some rocket dressed with lemon, and slices of parmesan.

### PANINI CON PORCHETTA

*Roll filled with roast pork and radicchio*

In Italy you can buy your roast pork from little bars on the side of the road; in Australia, I suggest you keep some leftover from dinner. Split the bread roll in half and brush with a little extra-virgin olive oil. Add thin slices of roast pork and a little crackling, then brush with hot mustard. Add some radicchio leaves dressed with lemon.

### PANINI ORTOLANO

*Roll filled with grilled garden vegetables*

Barbecue some vegetables such as red peppers, eggplants and zucchini. Split the bread roll in half and brush with pesto. Cover pesto with basil leaves and then add the vegetables. Finish with a squeeze of lemon and some provolone cheese.

### PANINI AL POMODORO

*Roll with squashed tomatoes and basil*

Split the bread roll in half and brush with a little extra-virgin olive oil. Lightly toast roll and rub with a halved garlic clove. Add some basil leaves and another drizzle of extra-virgin olive oil. Squash a ripe tomato onto the bread and finish with a little salt.

Clockwise from top left: *panini san daniele, panini con porchetta, panini ortolano*

*Panini al pomodoro*

# Tramezzini

## ITALIAN CRUSTLESS SANDWICHES

This great bar snack reminds me of Harry's Bar in Venice.

Bring a saucepan of water to the boil and add eggs. Cook for 3–4 minutes, or until soft-boiled, then drain, peel and set aside.

Bring another saucepan of salted water to the boil. Trim asparagus spears and add to water. Cook for 2–3 minutes, or until tender. Drain, allow to cool, then finely chop.

In a bowl, mash eggs then add asparagus spears, mayonnaise, lemon juice, chives and anchovies, and season with salt and pepper. Mix well.

Cut 4 thick (2–3 cm) slices of bread and lay flat. Spread filling over two slices of bread, adding a little more in the centre (like a small mound). Top with remaining bread and trim the crusts off.

**Serves 2**

**4 free-range eggs**

**1 bunch asparagus spears**

**100 g mayonnaise**

**juice of ½ lemon**

**½ bunch finely chopped chives**

**4 anchovy fillets in oil, finely chopped**

**sea salt and freshly ground black pepper**

**400–500 g square-loaf bread, unsliced**

Makes 2 large
(30–40 cm) pizzas

**for pizza speck**

**1 quantity basic pizza dough
(see recipe on page 168)**

**1¼ cups *sugo di pomodoro*
(see recipe on page 47)**

**10 basil leaves, torn**

**sea salt and freshly ground
black pepper**

**20 very thin slices speck
(pancetta)**

**400 g fresh mozzarella,
sliced or broken**

**extra-virgin olive oil,
for drizzling**

**for pizza *cicoria***

**1 quantity basic pizza dough
(see recipe on page 168)**

**1 large bunch chicory, washed
and roughly chopped**

**olive oil, for cooking**

**1 large Spanish onion,
finely chopped**

**4 cloves garlic, finely chopped**

**1 teaspoon dried chilli**

**sea salt and freshly ground
black pepper**

**300g fresh mozzarella, sliced**

**extra-virgin olive oil,
for drizzling**

**for pizza prosciutto**

**1 quantity basic pizza dough
(see recipe on page 168)**

**1¼ cups *sugo di pomodoro*
(see recipe on page 47)**

**10 basil leaves, torn**

**sea salt and freshly ground
black pepper**

**400 g fresh mozzarella,
sliced or broken**

**20 very thin slices prosciutto**

# My three favourite pizzas: speck (pancetta), *cicoria* (chicory) and prosciutto

Preheat oven to 240°C.

Lightly oil two large baking trays (the shape doesn't matter). On a bench, roll pizza dough to 1 cm thickness, then cut to fit trays. Lay dough on trays.

### FOR PIZZA SPECK

Spread tomato sauce evenly over dough to coat. Arrange basil leaves over tomato, and lightly season with salt and pepper. (Remember that cured meats are salty, so you will only need a little salt.) Arrange speck slices over pizza, then lay slices or broken pieces of mozzarella over top, and bake for 10–12 minutes, or until pizza base is crispy. Finish with a drizzle of extra-virgin olive oil.

### FOR PIZZA *CICORIA*

Bring a large saucepan of salted water to the boil and add chicory. Cook for 4–5 minutes, or until just tender.

In a heavy-based frying pan, heat olive oil over low heat and fry onion and garlic until soft. Add chicory and chilli, and season with salt and pepper. Fry gently, stirring until all ingredients are well mixed. Remove from heat and allow to cool.

Spread mozzarella over pizza base and evenly spread chicory mixture over the top. Bake for 10–15 minutes, or until pizza base is crispy. Finish with a drizzle of extra-virgin olive oil.

### FOR PIZZA PROSCIUTTO

Spread tomato sauce evenly over dough to coat. Arrange basil leaves over tomato, then lay slices or broken pieces of mozzarella over basil leaves and lightly season with salt and pepper. (Remember that cured meats are salty, so you will only need a little salt.) Bake for 10–12 minutes, or until pizza base is crispy, then remove from oven and arrange a thin layer of prosciutto over mozzarella.

For a special finish, make a rocket salad dressed with lemon juice and olive oil, and lay it over prosciutto pizza before serving.

Left to right: *pizza speck, pizza cicoria, pizza prosciutto*

# Polenta chips

Serves 4

250 g polenta

250 g semolina

1.5 litres water

100 g butter

sea salt

cottonseed oil,
for frying

sour cream or sea salt,
to serve

Polenta chips are a Melbourne Wine Room favourite, thanks to Karen Martini. They are the perfect accompaniment to a glass of wine or beer.

In a bowl, mix polenta and semolina together.

Pour water into a large, heavy-based saucepan, then add butter and salt and bring to the boil. Sprinkle in polenta mixture while whisking continuously. Whisk until mixture is smooth and thick. Reduce heat to low and cook for 5 minutes, stirring constantly.

Pour mixture into an oiled tray to 2.5 cm thickness and smooth over with a spatula. Chill for at least 2 hours, then cut into 6 cm × 2 cm wedges.

Heat oil in a deep saucepan over very high heat. (To test oil, add a polenta chip or a piece of stale bread; it should sizzle immediately.) When oil is ready, add polenta chips in small batches and fry for 6–8 minutes, or until crispy on the outside and hot on the inside. Once chips are ready, add each batch to a warm oven on a tray lined with absorbent paper.

Serve in a large bowl with a side dish of sour cream or sea salt.

# Pizza fritta

FRIED PIZZA

Serves 4

**1 quantity basic pizza dough
(see recipe on page 168)**

**100 ml olive oil**

**salt or caster sugar, to serve**

Whether you have it savoury or sweet, this dish shouts of summer
in Italy. Enjoy it with sugar in the morning, or with salt in the evening.
My mother still spoils me with this dish, and my son, Sylvester, loves
it with some prosciutto.

Divide pizza dough into 12 balls and flatten each ball into a 6–8 cm disc. Cut a
slit about 2 cm long into the middle of each pizza. (This will fill with oil and allow
the dough to cook evenly.) In a heavy-based frying pan, heat oil over medium
heat. Add 3–4 pizzas at a time and cook for a few minutes on each side, until
golden brown. Sprinkle with either salt or sugar (or top with prosciutto) and
serve immediately (once cold, *pizza fritta* will go rock hard).

# Salmon rillette

Serves 4–6

**500 g salmon fillet**

**100 g softened
unsalted butter**

**75 g plain yoghurt**

**2 free-range egg yolks**

**50 ml extra-virgin olive oil**

**juice of 1 lemon**

**sea salt and freshly ground
black pepper**

**½ bunch finely chopped chives**

This recipe is from Karen Martini. Served with crusty bread or crackers,
it makes a great snack. To save yourself time and hassle, ask your
fishmonger to bone, skin and clean your salmon.

Remove skin, bloodline and bones from salmon fillet, and cut in half lengthways.

In a bowl, whisk butter until light and creamy, then add yoghurt and egg yolks
and continue whisking until mixture is glossy. Drizzle in oil and set aside.

Place salmon in a frying pan, then add enough water to cover salmon. Add a
squeeze of lemon juice – set remaining juice aside – and season with salt and
pepper. Place pan over low heat and simmer for 6 minutes, or until centre of
fish is pink. Remove salmon from liquid and strain, then set aside to cool to
room temperature.

Gently remove any remaining bloodline and bones from salmon. Flake salmon,
collecting juice in a bowl. Add salmon to butter mix and add chives, remaining
lemon juice and salmon juice. Season with salt and pepper, gently folding
through. Serve immediately.

 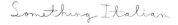

*Pizza fritta*

# Essential snacks

Growing up in Italy, when my mother was cooking dinner and we were a little hungry, we liked to have a small starter or snack. During summer we used to eat tomatoes on bread every day – how could we survive without it? Try some of my favourites . . .

### bruschetta

Get some really ripe tomatoes – and I mean really ripe, voluptuous tomatoes – and a piece of crusty sourdough bread. Toast the bread until golden brown and then rub it with a halved garlic clove. Squash the tomato in your fist and push it down onto the bread – the bread will suck up all the flavour. Add a little salt and a drizzle of virgin olive oil. Perfection!

### mozzarella

Cut some mozzarella into 3 cm cubes and place on a skewer. (Add as many pieces as you like, keeping them flush up against each other.) Drizzle a little extra-virgin olive oil over the mozzarella. I like to cook these on a really hot barbecue until just golden brown and starting to melt. When your mozzarella is ready, squeeze over a little lemon juice and season with salt and pepper. You must eat them hot. (Alternatively, you can lightly coat your cheese pieces in a crumbing mix and fry them in extra-virgin olive oil on the stove over medium heat.)

### chocolate

What kid (or adult) doesn't like Nutella? Simply smear masses of Nutella on soft slices of Vienna loaf or a sweet bread such as brioche or *panini al latte* (see recipe on page 28). Nutella is also great smothered all over pancakes for breakfast.

### prosciutto

Prosciutto should always be fresh and sliced thinly just prior to use – if sliced too far in advance, it loses its moisture and salty flavour. Prosciutto can be wrapped around just about any food, such as *grissini* (see recipe on page 181), sliced figs, fresh mozzarella, or cooked green beans dressed with balsamic vinegar. The options are endless.

## artichokes

This is so simple. Cook marinated artichokes under a griller or on a hot barbecue and serve drizzled with a little lemon juice.

## oysters

You must buy oysters closed – you eat oysters to taste the sea, and when they are sold open they have been washed in water – and it is therefore essential to learn how to open them. Simply shuck and detach them from the shell, squeeze a little lemon juice over and slurp away. As a variation, try some salmon roe and lemon juice with the oysters. (Oysters can be kept in your refrigerator for 2–5 days with a damp cloth over them so they don't get too cold and die. If they smell, don't eat them – they are dead.)

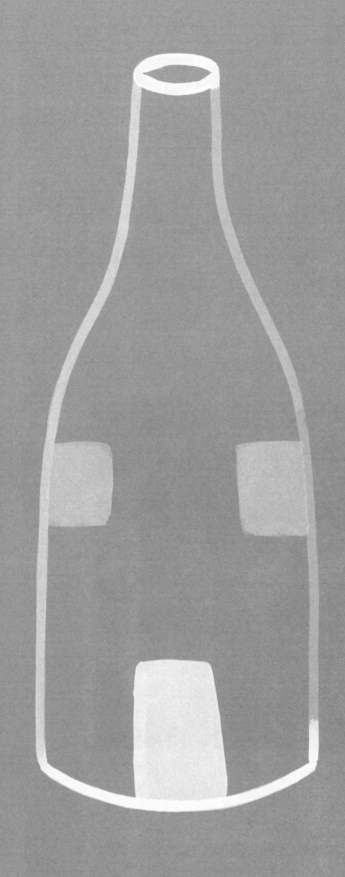

Cena

Dinner in Italy is very family driven, and is usually eaten at home rather than in a restaurant. That's what these recipes will give you: a taste of Italy at home.

We always served two courses for dinner, but they were not served formally as an entrée and a main course. We tended to adopt the idea of a single, feasting menu. When I cook for friends, I love to put all the food on the table at once and then sit down with everyone to eat and enjoy.

There has not been much experimentation over the years in Italian cooking, which is why some of our regular dishes are just as loved today as they were when we first put them on the Caffé e Cucina menu in 1988. Italians have been eating the same types of food for generations because the ingredients are good, core ingredients that don't need to be played around with. Cooking techniques have changed — we no longer feel a compulsion to overcook everything like my parents did — but the basic ingredients are the same.

Dinner is usually the meal that you have the most time to prepare for and the most time to sit down and enjoy, therefore you enjoy it in a different way. I tend to experiment a little bit more with dinner for these reasons. It's about the food complementing your social gathering and conversation.

# Pollo alla Maurizio

## MAURIZIO'S CHICKEN

Serves 2–4

2 kg whole organic
chicken, butterflied

100 g fresh rosemary,
roughly chopped

4 bay leaves

1 onion, sliced

2 lemons, sliced

3 potatoes, sliced

juice of 2 lemons

100 ml balsamic vinegar

sea salt and freshly ground
black pepper

200 ml olive oil

This dish has never been on any of my menus but it is very classic, simple and tasty – pay a little more for a good chook, because it is worth it. Ask your butcher to cut down the backbone and butterfly the chicken.

Preheat oven to 220°C.

In a bowl, combine rosemary, bay leaves, onion, potato, lemon slices, the juice from 1 lemon and balsamic vinegar, and season with salt and pepper.

Lay potato mix in a heavy, ovenproof dish. Lay chicken on top and drizzle oil over chicken, then sprinkle with salt and pepper. Bake for 35 – 45 minutes, or until cooked. (To test chicken, insert a skewer under a leg – if the juices run clear, the chicken is ready.)

Remove chicken from baking dish, cut into desired portions and place on a serving platter. Remove all fat from baking dish and place baking dish over low heat. Add juice of remaining lemon, and stir to deglaze dish, scraping all the goodies from the base. Pour liquid over chicken, then garnish with some of the rosemary from inside the chicken.

# Quaglie brasate con pancetta

## BRAISED QUAIL WRAPPED IN PANCETTA

**Serves 4**

**100 g dried porcini mushrooms**

**8 large quail, partly boned with leg and thigh still attached (ask your butcher to do this for you)**

**sea salt and freshly ground black pepper**

**14 sprigs thyme**

**15 very thin slices aged pancetta**

**120 ml olive oil**

**5 cloves garlic, chopped**

**75 g unsalted butter**

**900 ml red wine**

**200 ml chicken stock (see recipe on page 180)**

This is Robert Marchetti's wonderful, modern twist on the Roman classic *saltimbocca alla Romana*. This dish goes well with *polenta* (see recipe on page 175).

Place porcini mushrooms in a bowl and cover with water. Set aside to soak for 40 minutes.

Preheat oven to 240°C.

Drain mushrooms and set aside, reserving the cooking liquid for later.

Season quail with salt and pepper. Wrap each quail with a sprig of thyme and a slice of pancetta. Push a skewer through the middle of each quail to fasten the pancetta.

In a frying pan, heat oil and add quail. Sear until golden, ensuring pancetta remains attached to quail. Transfer quail to a plate and set aside. Add garlic, butter, mushrooms and remaining thyme to pan. Cook gently (do not allow to brown) until soft, then add porcini liquid and stir to deglaze pan. Continue cooking (but don't stir) until liquid has reduced to a thick sauce. Transfer to a baking dish and add quail. Pour in wine and seal with a lid. Bake for 10 minutes, or until quail is cooked pink.

Remove quail from oven. (If the sauce needs to be thickened further, stir over a low heat until suitably reduced.) Check seasoning and set aside to cool.

When quail has cooled, remove skewers and cut quail into desired portions. Return quail to the frying pan. Add chicken stock and heat through. Serve with rice.

This dish will keep, refrigerated, for 5–6 days.

# Poached tuna niçoise

This dish, by Robert Marchetti, is a much better alternative to tinned tuna. You need a pressure cooker to make this dish.

Heat oil in a pressure cooker and add carrot, celery, onion, peppercorns and bay leaves. Sauté until soft. Add wine, reduce heat and simmer for 10 minutes, or until liquid has reduced to a glaze. Add stock and season with salt and pepper, then bring mixture to the boil. Add tuna and place lid on pressure cooker. As soon as pressure has been obtained, turn off heat, release steam cap without removing, then immerse pan in iced water. (Don't let the iced water rise above the lid.)

When steam is gone and pan is cold, remove lid and transfer tuna and cooking liquid to separate bowls. Refrigerate both bowls (do not cover), allowing them to cool. When liquid is cold, pour into a large bowl. Add lemon juice, then season with salt and pepper.

Once chilled, the tuna can be covered with the liquid and kept, refrigerated, for 2–3 weeks. You can use it just like tinned tuna, in salads or sandwiches.

**Serves 4**

**1 ⅓ cups olive oil**

**2 large carrots, roughly chopped**

**2 sticks celery, roughly chopped**

**2 large onions, roughly chopped**

**5 peppercorns**

**2 bay leaves**

**200 ml white wine**

**2 cups fish stock (see recipe on page 180)**

**sea salt and freshly ground black pepper**

**½ side (approximately 2 kg) tuna**

**juice of 1 lemon**

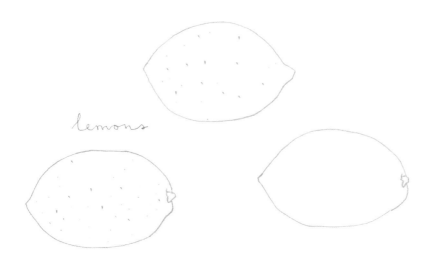

lemons

# Pallaiard alla milanese

## THIN ESCALOPE OF VEAL GRILLED WITH BASIL

Serves 2

**2 × 250 g piece thin veal
(ask your butcher to
leave the bone on)**

**400 g basil, finely chopped**

**350 ml extra-virgin olive oil**

**2 handfuls rocket**

**juice of 1 lemon**

**sea salt and freshly ground
black pepper**

**1 lemon, halved**

This is incredibly simple and is great for a quick meal.

Place veal on a plate and smother on both sides with basil and half the oil. Refrigerate for 20 minutes to marinate.

Heat barbecue to its hottest temperature, then add veal and cook for 2 minutes on each side.

While veal is cooking, add rocket to a bowl with lemon juice and remaining oil, and season with salt and pepper.

Arrange on a plate with halved lemon and serve with salad.

# Agnello alla griglia con rosmarino

## GRILLED LAMB WITH ROSEMARY

Serves 2

**2 × 200 g lamb fillets (loins)**

**200 ml extra-virgin olive oil**

**2 cloves garlic, thinly sliced**

**2 sprigs rosemary**

**sea salt and freshly ground
black pepper**

**handful rocket leaves**

**1 lemon, halved**

Place lamb in a bowl and pour oil over to coat meat. Add garlic to bowl. Season rosemary leaves with salt and pepper, then tear and add to bowl. Set lamb aside to marinate for 2 hours.

Heat barbecue to its hottest temperature, then add lamb and cook for 3–4 minutes on each side. Remove from heat (keeping juices) and allow to rest for 2 minutes (this allows lamb to remain tender). Slice lamb into thin strips and serve dressed in its juices with rocket and halved lemon.

*Pallaiard alla milanese*

# Ribollita

## TUSCAN VEGETABLE SOUP

**Serves 4**

**125 g cannelloni beans (dried or fresh)**

**125 g borlotti beans (dried or fresh)**

**2 tablespoons bicarbonate of soda**

**1 large tomato**

**½ bulb garlic**

**handful fresh sage**

**200 ml olive oil**

**1 large bunch flat-leaf parsley, chopped**

**4 cloves garlic, finely chopped**

**2 bunches celery, chopped into 3–4 cm pieces**

**450 g carrots, chopped into 3–4 cm pieces**

**4 medium-sized Spanish onions, chopped into 3–4 cm pieces**

**2 × 425 g cans peeled tomatoes, drained**

**2 kg black cabbage or silverbeet, roughly chopped**

**2 loaves stale ciabatta bread with crusts torn off**

**50 ml extra-virgin olive oil**

**sea salt and freshly ground black pepper**

This is Robert Marchetti's Tuscan interpretation of the classic minestrone soup. You will need to prepare the beans a day before serving.

Place beans in a large bowl and cover with lots of water. Add bicarbonate of soda and soak overnight.

Drain beans well. Place in a saucepan and cover with fresh water. Bring to the boil, then reduce heat and simmer for 10 minutes. Drain again. Cover beans with fresh water and add tomato, garlic and sage. Place over low heat and simmer, skimming to remove impurities, for 40 minutes, or until beans are tender. Remove from heat and transfer beans and cooking liquid to separate bowls. Set aside.

Heat olive oil in a large, deep frying pan. Add parsley, garlic, celery, carrot and onion and fry gently for about 30 minutes, or until the flavours combine. Add tomatoes and cook for a further 30 minutes. Add cabbage and half the beans with enough of their liquid to cover. Simmer for 30 minutes.

Place remaining beans in the bowl of an electric mixer. Purée beans, then return to soup with just enough boiling water to make the soup liquid.

Break bread into 5 cm strips. Add bread and extra-virgin olive oil to soup, and season with salt and pepper to serve.

# Zuppa di carciofo, porro e patata

## JERUSALEM ARTICHOKE, LEEK AND POTATO SOUP

This is another of Robert Marchetti's soups.

Serves 6–8

In a large saucepan, heat butter and oil over low heat, then add onion, artichoke, potato and leek and sauté for 4–6 minutes, or until vegetables are soft. Add wine and stir to deglaze pan. Add stock, and season with salt and pepper. Cook for 25–30 minutes, ensuring vegetables do not lose colour. When mixture has thickened, remove from heat and transfer to a food processor. Mix on high until soup is slightly chunky. Season with more salt and pepper if desired, and allow to cool.

Serve with black pepper and a drizzling of extra-virgin olive oil.

You can refrigerate this soup for 2–3 days.

**250 g butter**

**250 ml olive oil**

**4 large onions, finely chopped**

**2 kg Jerusalem artichokes, peeled and finely chopped**

**2 kg potatoes, finely chopped**

**2 kg leeks, finely chopped**

**200 ml white wine**

**5 litres chicken stock (see recipe on page 180)**

**sea salt and freshly ground black pepper**

**extra-virgin olive oil**

artichoke

# Crayfish salad à la Russe

This dish of Karen Martini's is a family favourite that she learnt from her grandmother. Over the years she has developed the recipe, adding her own touches and making it into a very luscious salad. The truffle oil can be further enhanced by the use of fresh truffles if you are feeling truly decadent.

Most of the work can be done hours before, leaving just the assembly to a few moments before serving; your guests will be stunned by the perception of effortless preparation. Enjoy with a bottle of champagne.

Live crayfish is the best option, but if it is not available (or if you prefer not to buy live), buy fresh crayfish.

## TO PREPARE CRAYFISH

If you have bought a fresh crayfish, move on to the next step. If you are using a live crayfish, chill it in the freezer for 1½ hours, or until crayfish is asleep.

Bring a large, deep saucepan of well-salted water to the boil. Add crayfish and the sliced lemon and boil for 20 minutes. Remove from heat and refresh (dunk) crayfish in cold water to stop the cooking process.

Using a sharp knife, remove head and cut it in half; scrape out orange mustard and set aside in a bowl. Cut crayfish in half starting at the head and finishing at the tail. Remove legs and crack them open to remove meat; place meat in a separate bowl. Starting at the tail end of the shell, cut underside of shell on both sides and gently remove flesh; add flesh to second bowl. Pour the juice of 1 lemon and the truffle oil over flesh, then cover and keep at room temperature.

## TO MAKE DRESSING

In a bowl, combine reserved crayfish mustard with garlic, mayonnaise, yoghurt and juice of remaining lemon. Season with salt and pepper, and set aside.

## TO MAKE VEGETABLE SALAD

Bring two saucepans of salted water to the boil. In the first pan, add potato, turnip, celeriac and carrot. Cook for 5–6 minutes, or until tender, then drain well. ➤

Serves 6
(entrée portions)

crayfish

1 x 1.5–1.8 kg green crayfish

3 lemons (one sliced, two juiced separately)

180 ml truffle oil

dressing

1 large clove garlic, finely chopped

125 g whole-egg mayonnaise

150 g natural thickened yoghurt

sea salt and freshly ground black pepper

vegetable salad

4 large potatoes, finely chopped

6 large turnips, cut into 1 cm cubes

1 large celeriac, cut into 1 cm cubes

4 large carrots, cut into 1 cm cubes

12 spears white asparagus, sliced

300 g peas

2 heads witlof

1 bunch chives, finely chopped

1 head celery leaves

extra-virgin olive oil, for drizzling

2 hard-boiled free-range eggs, grated

Meanwhile, in the second pan, add asparagus and cook for 1 minute, then add peas and cook both for a further 2 minutes. Drain well.

In a large bowl, combine all vegetables, then add crayfish meat. Mix and then fold through three-quarters of the dressing.

TO SERVE

In a bowl, combine all ingredients.

On a large platter, arrange crayfish shell. Lay all ingredients in shell and serve with lemon.

# Pesce alla griglia

## GRILLED FISH

Serves 2

**1 generous serve of your favourite fish (either fillets or whole)**

**sea salt and freshly ground black pepper**

**extra-virgin olive oil, for drizzling**

**1 lemon**

**handful parsley**

My feelings on fish are basic: keep it fresh and simple. I have always preferred to buy good-quality fish and serve it on its own, allowing the product to stand out, than prepare it in any fancy way. Not many restaurants have the courage to do this, and we received some criticism when we first began serving fish this way at Caffé e Cucina (our clients would ask, 'What else comes with it? No sauce?'), but you should take the chance; you will be delighted with the result. I love simple grilled fish, but you can serve it with a crisp salad, *spinaci saltati* (see recipe on page 176), *salsa verde* (see recipe on page 169) or *salsa di pomodoro* (see recipe on page 174).

Heat a griller or barbecue.

Lightly coat fish with a little salt and pepper. Grill or barbecue fish until slightly opaque in the centre, then remove from heat and drizzle with a little extra-virgin olive oil. Squeeze lemon juice over fish and sprinkle parsley around.

*Pesce alla griglia*

# Trippa alla parmigiana

## TRIPE IN THE STYLE OF PARMA

**Serves 4–6**

75 g dried borlotti beans

500 g honeycomb tripe

1 cotechino sausage
(available from butchers)

25 g dried porcini mushrooms

50 ml olive oil

125 g dried pancetta

250 g onions, finely chopped

175 g carrots, finely chopped

2 cloves garlic, chopped

1 small red chilli, chopped

dash of white-wine vinegar

180 ml dry white wine

150 ml beef stock

150 g *salsa di pomodoro*
(see recipe on page 174)

200 g tomato paste

1 teaspoon chopped oregano

1 teaspoon chopped basil

1 bay leaf

sea salt and freshly ground
black pepper

grated fresh parmesan,
to serve

Robert Marchetti's tripe is great with *polenta* (see recipe on page 175), *spinaci saltati* (see recipe on page 176) or potato mash (see recipe on page 175).

Place beans in a large bowl, cover with water and soak for 8–12 hours.

Transfer beans and their soaking liquid to a deep saucepan. Bring to the boil and cook for 30–45 minutes, or until tender.

In another large, deep saucepan, bring salted water to the boil. Add tripe and boil for 30–40 minutes, or until completely cooked and soft. Strain tripe into a colander and place a plate and a heavy weight on top. Leave for approximately 30 minutes, or until tripe is dry, then cut tripe into 7 cm x 1 cm strips.

Meanwhile, bring another saucepan of water to the boil and add cotechino sausage. Boil for 50 minutes, then remove from heat, drain and allow to cool. Cut into bite-sized cubes.

Place porcini mushrooms in a bowl, cover with warm water and soak for 30 minutes. Transfer mushrooms to a bowl and set liquid aside. Rinse mushrooms to remove grit, then chop and set aside.

Heat oil in a heavy-based frying pan and add pancetta. Sauté until crisp, then add onion and cook until translucent. Add porcini mushrooms, carrot, garlic and chilli and sauté for 10–15 minutes, or until vegetables are very soft. Add vinegar and scrape pan to deglaze. Reduce heat and simmer until liquid has reduced slightly. Add wine and simmer until liquid has reduced by two-thirds. Add tripe, then pour in just enough stock to cover to 1–2 cm from top of tripe. (Be careful not to add too much liquid, otherwise it will dilute the flavour.) Bring to the boil, then add tomato salsa, tomato paste, oregano, basil and bay leaf, and season with salt and pepper.

Reduce heat and simmer for 20–30 minutes, or until all ingredients are cooked. Add cooked beans and simmer for a further 10 minutes. Remove from heat and check seasoning. Serve on a large platter with parmesan.

# Insalata di saltimbocca di quaglia

## QUAIL SALTIMBOCCA

We perfected this at Otto. I once had this dish in Italy, done a little differently without the pear, but I love both versions.

Lay 2 slices of prosciutto per quail on a flat surface. Lay each quail skin-side down on corresponding prosciutto slices. Lay 2 sage leaves on the leg of each quail. Tightly wrap prosciutto around each quail from head to tail.

Heat olive oil in a large, non-stick frying pan over medium heat and add wrapped quail. Fry for 2–3 minutes on each side, until golden brown. (Do not move quail around the pan too much, otherwise they will stew rather than brown.) (If your quail is not boned, split it in half and cook for 2–3 minutes longer on each side.) Remove quail from heat and set aside in a warm place.

In a bowl, arrange radicchio and pear. Dress with a little extra-virgin olive oil and balsamic vinegar, and season with salt and pepper. Arrange salad on a serving plate and place quail on top. Finish with a little more extra-virgin olive oil, and serve with lemon wedges.

**Serves 4**

**20 thin slices prosciutto**

**4 jumbo quail
(ask your butcher to
butterfly and bone them)**

**20 sage leaves**

**100 ml olive oil**

**2 heads radicchio, leaves
separated**

**1 brown-skinned pear,
chopped to 1 cm cubes**

**100–200 ml extra-virgin
olive oil**

**100 ml apple balsamic vinegar
(you can use plain balsamic
vinegar if apple balsamic
vinegar is not available)**

**sea salt and freshly ground
black pepper**

**1 lemon, sliced into wedges**

pears

# Pesce spada di Romagna

## BREADED SWORDFISH WITH
## A SALAD OF TOMATO AND ROCKET

Serves 2

100 g plain flour

2 free-range eggs

sea salt and freshly ground
black pepper

200 g coarse breadcrumbs

¼ bunch flat-leaf parsley,
finely chopped

¼ bunch mint, finely chopped

finely grated zest of ½ lemon

2 × 200 g swordfish steaks
(if fresh swordfish is
unavailable, use fresh tuna)

2 handfuls rocket

¼ bunch basil, leaves picked

2 ripe tomatoes, finely
chopped

juice of 1 lemon

100 ml extra-virgin olive oil

200 ml olive oil

½ lemon, cut into wedges

You will need three large bowls. In the first, place flour. In the second, lightly beat eggs with a little salt and pepper. In the third, combine breadcrumbs, parsley, mint and lemon zest, and season with salt and pepper.

Lightly coat swordfish steaks with flour, then dip in egg, then coat with breadcrumbs.

In a separate bowl, combine rocket, basil, tomato, lemon juice and extra-virgin olive oil, and season with salt and pepper. Mix well.

Heat olive oil in a heavy-based frying pan over medium heat. Add swordfish and fry gently for 1–2 minutes on each side, or until golden brown. Remove and place on absorbent paper to drain.

Arrange salad on serving plates then arrange swordfish steaks and lemon over salad to serve.

# Chargrilled salt-crusted rib eye

This dish, by Karen Martini, was a favourite at The Melbourne Wine Room and is now also loved by my clients at Icebergs. To make it, you will need a Weber filled with coal (Mallee root coal is ideal), peaking at its hottest point when cooking begins. The rib eye cannot be cooked on a briquette barbecue because the heat needs to be intense to seal the crust, otherwise it will overcook. Go all out and buy a good piece of meat; tell your butcher what it is for. Ask your butcher to ensure the meat has even marbling and fat remaining.

Heat Weber to the highest possible temperature.

On a baking tray, sprinkle salt and white pepper to approximately 5 mm thickness, and set aside in a place near the grill.

Place rib eye on the hottest part of the grill and seal for 5–6 minutes on each side. Transfer to tray and rest for a minimum of 15 minutes, turning the meat once so the seasoning covers both sides. Meanwhile, keep grill hot.

Return rib eye to grill and cook to desired doneness. When rib eye is about 2 minutes from being ready, transfer to tray and leave to rest (it will continue to cook on the tray) for 2 minutes. (Resting the meat is important for tenderness.)

Remove rib eye from tray and cut into thick slices (or leave whole, if you prefer). Arrange on serving plates, drizzle with olive oil and squeeze lemon juice over. Serve with potato mash (see recipe on page 175).

Serve with potato mash (see recipe on page 175).

Serves 2
hungry people

**200 g Sicilian sea salt (Sicilian is finer-grained than standard sea salt)**

**2 tablespoons freshly ground white pepper**

**2 × 500 g rib eye, at room temperature**

**250 ml extra-virgin olive oil**

**2 lemons, halved**

# Capesante al forno

## BAKED SCALLOPS

Serves 4

¼ bulb garlic

200 g cooked borlotti beans

400 g bulb fennel, finely chopped

1 cup fennel tops, roughly chopped

120 g green olives, stoned and roughly chopped

50 g mustard fruits

100 ml aged red-wine vinegar

100 ml extra-virgin olive oil

sea salt and freshly ground black pepper

20 scallops, left in their half-shells

extra-virgin olive oil, for drizzling

Freshly cooked borlotti beans have a better flavour than canned ones, but you can use the canned variety if fresh are not available. You must, however, use fresh scallops – if you can't get them, you would be better off making a bowl of pasta!

Preheat oven to 160°C.

Place garlic on an oven tray and bake slowly for 20 minutes, or until soft and mushy. Remove from oven, allow to cool and then discard skins. With a fork, mash garlic to a paste.

Increase oven temperature to 180°C.

In a bowl, combine beans, fennel, fennel tops and olives. In a separate bowl, combine mashed garlic, mustard fruits and vinegar. Slowly drizzle in oil, and season with salt and pepper. Pour this dressing over bean salad, and set aside.

Lay scallops on a baking tray and drizzle with a little extra-virgin olive oil, and season with salt and pepper. Bake scallops for 2–3 minutes, or until opaque. Remove scallops and dress generously with the scallop juice and bean salad to serve.

# Guazzetto di pesce con fregola e finocchio

## FISH STEW WITH PASTA AND FENNEL

**fennel fish stock**

**40 ml olive oil**

**6 large onions,
roughly chopped**

**3 sticks celery,
roughly chopped**

**6 cloves garlic, roughly
chopped**

**2 bulbs fennel,
roughly chopped**

**3 carrots, roughly chopped**

**4 kg fish bones, washed**

**200 g tomato paste**

**12 bay leaves**

**1 tablespoon peppercorns**

**80 ml Pernod**

**400 ml red wine**

**400 ml white wine**

**soup**

**4 blue swimmer crabs**

**8 scampi**

**1 kg whole calamari**

**1 kg whole mussels in shells,
cleaned and debearded**

**1 kg sea clams, washed**

**sea salt and freshly ground
black pepper**

**30 ml olive oil**

**200 g fregola (toasted pasta
granules – available from
fine food stores)**

**500 g yellow-fin tuna, cut into
bite-sized pieces**

**2.5 litres fennel fish stock**

**extra-virgin olive oil,
for drizzling**

The seafood suggested here can be replaced with scallops, prawns or oysters, and in any amounts. Have your fishmonger prepare your seafood for you.

### TO MAKE FENNEL FISH STOCK

Heat oil in a large, heavy-based frying pan over low heat. Add onion, celery, garlic, fennel and carrot and fry gently until soft (do not allow to brown). Add fish bones and fry for 15 minutes. Add tomato paste, bay leaves and peppercorns and fry for 10 minutes. Add Pernod, red wine and white wine and simmer to reduce liquid by two-thirds. Transfer ingredients to a stockpot and add 3 litres water, then bring to the boil. Reduce heat and simmer, skimming impurities that rise to the top, for 2 hours. (You should have 2.5 litres of liquid remaining.) Remove from heat, then strain and set aside to cool.

### TO PREPARE SEAFOOD

With a sharp, pointed knife, cut each crab into 4 pieces and set aside.

Halve scampi lengthways, then clean and wash out stomach and intestinal tract.

Remove skin from calamari. Remove mouth from tentacles and dice body and wings into 2.5 cm squares.

Mussels and clams need no further preparation.

### TO MAKE SOUP

Season seafood with salt and pepper.

Heat olive oil in a large frying pan over high heat. When oil is smoking, add seafood and seal on both sides. (Seafood such as oysters, scallops and scampi should be added after you add the fregola, 4 minutes before serving.) Add stock and bring to the boil, then add fregola. Simmer for 7 minutes, or until fregola is al dente.

Remove stew from heat and check seasoning. Pour into deep bowls, drizzle with extra-virgin olive oil and serve with grilled bread.

# Spezzatini di agnello con carciofi

## LAMB SHOULDER WITH ARTICHOKE-HEART SAUCE

Preheat oven to 170°C.

Bring a saucepan of well-salted water to the boil and add pasta. Cook until al dente, then drain and set aside to cool.

Peel outer leaves off artichokes until you reach yellow, tender leaves. Trim 5 mm from the top of artichoke and remove stalk. Cut artichokes in half from top to bottom, then place on an oiled baking tray. Bake for 20 minutes, remove from oven and set aside.

In a bowl, season flour with salt and pepper, then lightly dust lamb cubes. Heat a heavy-based frying pan with 100 ml of the oil over medium–high heat. When oil is very hot, add lamb and cook for 4–5 minutes, browning evenly. Remove lamb from pan, then drain and set aside.

Reduce heat to medium and, in the same pan, heat the remaining oil and the butter. Add eschalots, carrots, celery, garlic, oregano and bay leaf and fry gently for 5–6 minutes, or until soft. Add lamb and wine, then simmer until wine has completely reduced. Add stock, season with salt and pepper and simmer for 45 minutes. Add artichokes and simmer for a further 15 minutes. (The sauce should be of a thick consistency.) Add peas and cook for 2 minutes. Stir in pasta and parmesan, then stir in mint. Check seasoning and serve immediately.

Serves 4

**500 g tiny tubetti (or any small pasta)**

**10 artichokes**

**sea salt and freshly ground black pepper**

**150 g plain flour**

**1 kg lamb shoulder, cut into 2 cm cubes (ask your butcher to leave the fat on and trim the sinew)**

**200 ml olive oil**

**100 g butter**

**10 eschalots, peeled and sliced**

**6 Dutch carrots, peeled and thinly sliced (Dutch carrots are a little sweeter than standard carrots)**

**1 celery heart, finely chopped**

**5 cloves garlic, thinly sliced**

**3 sprigs oregano**

**1 fresh bay leaf**

**500 ml dry white wine**

**1.5 litres chicken stock (see recipe on page 180)**

**250 g peas**

**100 g grated fresh parmesan**

**3 sprigs mint, finely chopped**

oregano

# Lamb osso buco
# with Middle-Eastern spices

Serves 6–8

**5 kg lamb osso buco**

**4 tablespoons cumin salt**

**freshly ground black pepper**

**200 ml olive oil**

**6 onions, finely chopped**

**8 cloves garlic, finely chopped**

**5 sticks celery, finely chopped**

**½ bulb celeriac, finely chopped**

**3 bay leaves**

**6 sprigs thyme**

**200 g pancetta, broken into pieces**

**4 hot red chillies, chopped**

**5 hot green chillies, chopped**

**2 tablespoons ground coriander seeds, lightly toasted**

**½ bunch coriander with roots, washed and chopped**

**½ bunch flat-leaf parsley, roughly chopped**

**1.5 litres white wine**

**150 g tomato paste**

**150 g preserved lemon, chopped**

**1 litre chicken stock (see recipe on page 180)**

**2 × 425 g cans diced tomatoes**

This is a wonderful mix of Karen Martini's cooking and Italian food philosophies about simplicity and quality ingredients.

Season lamb with cumin salt and black pepper. In a large frying pan, add 100 ml of the oil and heat over low heat. Add lamb and cook for 4–6 minutes, or until meat is browned. Remove from heat, cover with foil and set aside.

In a separate frying pan, heat remaining oil over medium heat and add onion, garlic, celery, celeriac, bay leaves and thyme. Cook for 4–5 minutes, or until ingredients begin to caramelise. Add pancetta and chilli, and combine well. Add coriander seeds, coriander, parsley and lamb, and mix. Add wine, tomato paste and preserved lemon, and mix. Decrease heat and simmer for 10–15 minutes, or until all liquid has evaporated. Add stock and diced tomatoes and continue simmering for 40–50 minutes, or until lamb is well cooked.

Serve with grilled bread, yoghurt and a salad of preserved lemon, Spanish onion, parsley and coriander.

# Sardine fresche con cuore di sedani e noci

MARINATED SARDINES WITH CELERY HEARTS
AND WALNUTS

Serves 4

20 sardine fillets,
cleaned and boned (only use
fresh sardines, not frozen)

100 ml dry white wine

3 tablespoons olive oil

50 g walnuts, roughly chopped

2 celery hearts, finely chopped

sea salt and freshly ground
black pepper

This was one of our most popular dishes at Il Bàcaro – an Italian classic.

Preheat oven to 180°C.

In a baking tray, lay sardines out flat. Pour wine and oil over sardines, then sprinkle with walnuts and celery hearts, and season with salt and pepper. Bake for 5–6 minutes. Serve warm with a crisp salad.

# Blue cheese pannacotta

Serves 4

500 ml milk

300 ml cream

280 g gorgonzola cheese
(no rind), finely chopped

4 ½ leaves gelatine

sea salt and freshly ground
black pepper

Karen Martini created this dish at The Melbourne Wine Room. It shows off Mediterranean flavours . . . with a twist. It's great with some grissini (see recipe on page 181) and a crisp salad, and is a wonderful alternative to a cheese platter.

In a saucepan, stir milk and cream over medium heat to simmering point, then remove from heat. Pour mixture over cheese and whisk to melt cheese. Add gelatine and stir to dissolve. Season with salt and pepper, then strain through a fine strainer. Pour into a terrine dish (a 2-litre capacity is suitable) and refrigerate for 4–6 hours before serving. A little warm water around the outside of the dish will remove the pannacotta from its mould.

*Sardine fresche con cuore di sedani e noci*

# Zuppa di Pasqua

## GINA'S EASTER SOUP

**chicken broth**

4–5 kg whole organic chicken

1 large carrot

2 sticks celery

1 large brown onion,
roughly chopped

¼ bunch flat-leaf parsley

1 large ripe tomato

sea salt and freshly ground
black pepper

**chicken dumplings**

250 g finely minced chicken

2 tablespoons grated
fresh parmesan

150 g fresh breadcrumbs

1 free-range egg

3 tablespoons flat-leaf
parsley, finely chopped

600 ml olive oil

3 kg (approximately
1 bunch) chicory

**stracciatella mix**

2 free-range eggs

3 tablespoons grated
fresh parmesan

2 tablespoons flat-leaf
parsley, finely chopped

This is an old family recipe of my mother's. I can still remember my mother and aunts preparing the chicken dumplings – all rolled perfectly – for this dish for days before Easter. While growing up in Italy we enjoyed this dish at festive times, not just during Easter. We always knew it was a special day when Mum served this.

You will need to start preparing this dish well in advance. Cooking with organic ingredients will give you a better-tasting end product.

### TO MAKE CHICKEN BROTH

Place chicken in a heavy-based saucepan and cover with cold water. Place pan over high heat and bring to the boil. Ladle off any impurities that rise to the top, then add carrot, celery, onion, parsley and tomato. Reduce heat and simmer for 40 minutes, or until chicken is just cooked through (no pink should be left on the bone). Add a pinch of salt and pepper to taste, then remove pan from heat. Strain vegetables and chicken, keeping the broth. Discard chicken and vegetables, and refrigerate broth, covered, overnight.

Remove broth from refrigerator; all the fat should have risen and set on the top of the broth. Remove fat and discard. Set broth aside.

### TO MAKE CHICKEN DUMPLINGS

In a bowl, mix minced chicken, parmesan, breadcrumbs, egg and parsley until mixture becomes firm. Roll into small dumplings about the size of 10-cent coins.

Bring a saucepan of well-salted water to the boil. Meanwhile, clean chicory well, discarding any woody ends, and cut into bite-sized pieces. Add chicory to boiling water and cook for 5–10 minutes, or until tender. Remove and shock (dunk) in cold water to stop the cooking process.

Pour half the chicken broth in a deep saucepan and simmer over low heat for 20–30 minutes.

Meanwhile, in a deep frying pan, heat half the olive oil. When oil is hot (test by dropping a small piece of dumpling in; if it sizzles straight away, the oil is ready), add dumplings and fry for 3–5 minutes, or until lightly golden brown.

(Ensure you do not cook them right through – check by opening one of the dumplings.) Remove dumplings from oil and rinse under hot water to remove any excess oil. Place dumplings in simmering chicken broth and cook over low heat for around 30 minutes, or until cooked through and tender. Remove from pan and set aside. Reserve broth.

### TO MAKE STRACCIATELLA MIX

In a bowl, combine eggs, parmesan and parsley, and season with salt and pepper. Whisk ingredients together and set aside.

### TO SERVE

Bring remaining half of chicken broth to the boil in a saucepan. Add chicory, then reduce heat and simmer for 30 minutes.

In a large, deep saucepan, combine broths, chicken dumplings and chicory and bring to the boil. Add stracciatella mix and remove from heat. Stir well and check seasoning before serving.

eggs

# Anatra alla griglia

## BARBECUED DUCK LEGS

**Serves 2**

**2 duck legs**

**2 cloves garlic, crushed**

**100 ml balsamic vinegar**

**100 ml extra-virgin olive oil**

**½ bunch marjoram, roughly chopped**

**sea salt and freshly ground black pepper**

**2 lemon wedges**

This is a great dish to cook on the barbecue on a summer's night. You will need to prepare the duck the day before to allow the full flavour of the marinade to come through. It's great with *radicchio alla griglia e funghi alla griglia* (see recipe on page 171) or *spinaci saltati* (see recipe on page 176).

In a bowl, combine duck legs, garlic, vinegar, oil and marjoram, and season with salt and pepper. Marinate in refrigerator overnight.

Heat barbecue to a low heat. Place duck legs on barbecue and cook for 7–8 minutes each side. (Take care to cook the duck legs slowly so you don't burn the balsamic marinade.) Remove from heat and allow to rest. Serve duck at room temperature with lemon wedges.

 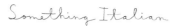

*Anatra alla griglia*, with *Radicchio alla griglia e funghi alla griglia* (see recipe on page 171)

# Salsiccie con funghi

## PORK SAUSAGES WITH MUSHROOM SAUCE

Robert Marchetti created this simple but fantastic meal.

Heat barbecue and cook sausages to desired doneness.

Heat butter and oil in a pan, then add mushrooms, garlic and onion and fry gently for 5–6 minutes, or until soft. Check seasoning and add salt and pepper as desired. Add wine and scrape pan to deglaze. Add balsamic vinegar and simmer for 2 minutes. Add cream and simmer gently for 3–4 minutes, or until thick and brown. Finish with parsley and basil if desired, and mix well. Pour sauce over sausages.

**Serves 2**

**4 coarse-textured pork sausages**

**50 g unsalted butter**

**50 ml olive oil**

**2 button mushrooms, sliced**

**2 shiitake mushrooms, sliced**

**2 abalone mushrooms, sliced**

**2 field mushrooms, sliced**

**2 chestnut mushrooms, sliced**

**2 cloves garlic, finely sliced**

**1 large onion, finely chopped**

**sea salt and freshly ground black pepper**

**100 ml dry white wine**

**50 ml aged balsamic vinegar**

**50 ml thickened cream**

**¼ bunch flat-leaf parsley, leaves picked (optional)**

**6 basil leaves, finely chopped (optional)**

# Chargrilled lamb cutlets with oregano and hot fetta dressing

**Serves 6**

3 × 8-cutlet racks of lamb (not Frenched)

6 cloves garlic, peeled

100 ml olive oil

juice of 1 lemon

1 tablespoon sherry vinegar

½ bunch fresh oregano, leaves picked

freshly ground black pepper

6 kipfler potatoes, scrubbed

extra-virgin olive oil, for drizzling

sea salt

200 g curly witlof

400 g pencil (small) leeks, trimmed, washed and cut into 5 cm sticks

120 ml lemon vinaigrette (see recipe on page 175)

80 g Ligurian-style olives

200 g soft fetta, marinated in oil (you can buy it already marinated)

This is a wonderful dish created by Karen Martini; it is full of Mediterranean flavours.

Leave a 1 cm layer of fat on lamb rack. With a sharp knife, score heavily into the fat in a crisscross pattern. Cut rack into cutlets.

With a mortar and pestle, smash garlic. Transfer garlic to a bowl and add oil, lemon juice, vinegar and half the oregano. Season with pepper and spread mixture over lamb.

Bring a saucepan of salted water to the boil. Slice potatoes lengthways to 1 cm thickness and add to pan. Boil for 4–6 minutes, or until tender. Drain potatoes, then drizzle a little extra-virgin olive oil over and season with salt and pepper. Place witlof in a bowl and toss potatoes through while still hot. Set aside in a warm place.

In a saucepan, bring water to the boil and add leeks. Cook for 2–3 minutes, then remove from heat and drain. Drizzle a little extra-virgin olive oil over while still hot, and season with salt and pepper.

Heat chargrill pan to a high heat. Season lamb cutlets with a little salt and then grill for 4–6 minutes each side, or until lightly browned.

While cutlets are cooking, heat a small saucepan over low heat and add vinaigrette, olives, fetta and remaining oregano. Stir gently to warm through.

Arrange warm potatoes and witlof on serving plates, then top with lamb cutlets and scatter leeks on top. Spoon hot fetta dressing over, and finish with extra grinds of black pepper.

# Galletto arrosto con ripieno di pane

## ROAST SPATCHCOCK WITH BREAD STUFFING

**Serves 4**

**4 cloves garlic**

**500 g sourdough bread**

**2 cloves garlic, extra, finely chopped**

**50 ml red-wine vinegar**

**sea salt**

**160 ml extra-virgin olive oil**

**½ bunch flat-leaf parsley, finely chopped**

**1 teaspoon mustard fruit paste (available from Italian delicatessens)**

**10 sage leaves, torn into bite-sized pieces**

**4 × 450 g spatchcocks (ask your butcher to remove the rib cage and wing tips, and to butterfly the spatchcocks for you)**

**200 g unsalted butter**

**4 teaspoons olive oil**

This is one of my all-time favourite spatchcock dishes, first made by Karen Martini at The Melbourne Wine Room.

Preheat oven to 160°C.

Place garlic on a baking tray and bake for 20 minutes, or until soft and mushy. Allow to cool, then discard skin and set garlic aside. Increase oven temperature to 200°C.

Heat griller on high. Cut bread into 1 cm-thick slices and toast for 4–5 minutes on both sides. Remove from heat and set aside to cool.

With a mortar and pestle, combine roasted garlic, finely chopped garlic, vinegar and a sprinkle of sea salt. Mix well until ingredients form a fine paste. Add extra-virgin olive oil, parsley, mustard fruit paste and sage leaves, and mix well. Tear toasted bread into bite-sized pieces and add to paste. Mix well, then use your hands to squeeze bread, ensuring it absorbs all the flavours. Set aside.

Lay each spatchcock skin-side up on your workbench. Gently place your fingers under the skin, starting at the back of the spatchcock, and slowly lift skin away from the meat, taking care not to rip the skin. (Do not take the skin off – you are simply making room for the stuffing.) Add 2 tablespoons of stuffing per spatchcock underneath the skin, ensuring that it mainly covers the breasts and back legs. (This will protect it from drying out, but take care not to put too much stuffing under the skin.) Weave a long wooden skewer through the back legs of each spatchcock, to seal the openings you made with your fingers.

In a heavy-based frying pan, heat 50 g of the butter and 1 teaspoon of olive oil over medium heat. When mixture begins to froth, add 1 spatchcock and fry for 3–4 minutes, turning to completely brown on both sides. Remove spatchcock from pan and place on an oiled baking tray. Wipe pan clean and repeat process until all spatchcocks are browned, using 50 g of the butter and 1 teaspoon olive oil each time.

Bake spatchcocks for 16–18 minutes, or until cooked. (To test spatchcock, insert a skewer under the main leg – if the juices run clear the spatchcock is ready.) Serve with a salad of rocket and lemon (see recipe on page 179).

# Zuppa di cavolfiore

## CAULIFLOWER SOUP

This is a delicious, smooth-based soup created by Robert Marchetti.

Cut cauliflower into 3 cm pieces. In a saucepan, heat oil over medium heat and add onion. Cook gently (but do not allow to brown) until glazed. Add cauliflower and cook slowly for 20–25 minutes, or until soft, then season with salt and pepper. Cover cauliflower and onion with cold water, then increase heat and simmer for approximately 30 minutes, or until mixture has coagulated. Allow to cool slightly, then transfer mixture to the bowl of an electric mixer. Purée mixture. Add cream if desired – double cream will give you a thicker, creamier texture. Check seasoning and add Pernod.

Before serving, return soup to saucepan and place over medium heat. Stir while heating, and mix through mascarpone to finish. (Ensure that you do not bring the mixture to the boil after you have added the mascarpone.)

You can keep this soup refrigerated in a sealed container for 3–4 days.

**Serves 4–6**

**2 large heads cauliflower**

**100 ml olive oil**

**3 large onions, sliced**

**sea salt and freshly ground white pepper**

**double cream (optional)**

**100 ml Pernod**

**200 g mascarpone**

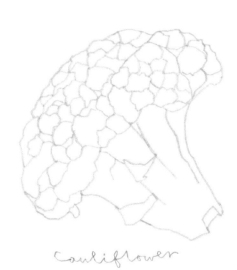

cauliflower

# Bistecca alla pizzaiola

## BEEF OR VEAL COOKED WITH A PIZZA SAUCE

This is a great late-night, last-minute meal – a bit like a mini steak. Heat a little olive oil in a frying pan over medium heat, and lightly fry some thin slices of beef or veal. Remove from heat and drain on absorbent paper. Lay meat on a plate and cover with a layer each of tomato sauce, sugar, black olives, fresh oregano leaves and buffalo mozzarella. Bake it all under the grill until the cheese melts.

# Maiale con prugne

## PORK CHOPS WITH PRUNES

Serves 2

2 thin slices bacon

4 prunes, pitted

1 tablespoon olive oil

1 tablespoon unsalted butter

2 × 240 g pork chops

175 ml dry white wine

1 teaspoon coarse-grained mustard

sea salt and freshly ground black pepper

Preheat oven to 180°C.

Line a baking tray with aluminium foil.

Cut each bacon slice lengthways in two. Wrap each prune in a slice of bacon, secure with a toothpick and arrange on foil. Bake for 10 minutes, or until bacon is crisp.

While prunes are baking, heat oil and butter in a frying pan over high heat. Add pork chops and cook for 3 minutes on each side. Remove pork from pan and place on a plate in oven to keep warm. Add wine and mustard to pan, and season with salt and pepper. Stir to combine ingredients with pan juices.

Arrange a pork chop on each plate, pour sauce over and top with 2 wrapped prunes (after removing toothpicks).

*Bistecca alla pizzaiola*

# Digestivo

In Italy, a very important part of dinner or lunch is *digestivo* (digestive), usually consumed after coffee. I have listed some of my favourites, which you can find in Italian specialty stores such as Enoteca Sileno in Carlton, Melbourne. Be careful, because some are quite alcoholic.

**Varnelli L'Anice Secco Speciale** A special dry aniseed liqueur made using a carefully guarded family recipe. It's best served on ice or with a dash of water.

**Varnelli Adesso** A liqueur made from anise and coffee. Best served neat, or for the ultimate indulgence, serve topped with thickened cream.

**Varnelli Amaro Sibilla** Made from a concoction of herbs and roots, and slightly sweetened with honey. It is best served neat as a digestive, or as an aperitif shaken with medium dry vermouth.

**Varnelli Amaro Tonica** An amaro carefully concocted from roots, herbs and honey. This is Varnelli's benchmark digestive and is recommended neat, to enjoy all its flavours.

**Pralina Amaro di Arancio** A liqueur made from an infusion of fruit and selected herbs that stimulates the gastric juices, acting as the perfect tonic. Recommended served over ice.

**Bergamino** The Bergamot is a very rare citrus fruit grown in Italy. Made using traditional methods, it is best consumed chilled.

**Ghentiane Astucciato Ecoforest** This liqueur is made from an infusion of the Genziana root. This creates a liquor of great benefit to digestion. It is best served chilled over ice.

**Amaro Nonino** A herbal infusion with a small part of aged aquavitae. Extraordinary fragrance of mountain herbs. Best served over ice or straight.

**Amaro Montenegro** A nutty lighter style amaro with a hint of sweetness. Best served over ice with an orange slice.

**Amaro Siciliano Averna** Still made from the same ancient recipe of herbs and roots. This amaro is bittersweet, and best enjoyed over ice with either lemon or orange.

**Fernet Branca** An infusion of over 40 herbs, this amaro is then aged in wooden casks. Best served neat.

**Cynar** Artichoke leaves and herbs are infused to make this low-alcohol digestive. Best served over ice or topped with soda.

**Jägermeister** Made from a secret recipe of 56 herbs and spices, Jägermeister's unique taste sets it apart from all other spirits. Best served frozen.

## Scroppino

Traditionally, Prosecco rather than vodka was the base flavour, mixed with cold lemon sorbet or granita. To make this drink with Prosecco, use the same recipe amount as given for vodka.

### Serves 4

**4 scoops sorbet (your favourite flavours)**

**120 ml vodka**

In a blender, add sorbet and vodka. Blend and pour into a frozen glass.

Dolce

To me, the day can begin and end with a sweet: a sweet patisserie for breakfast and a rich gelato after dinner.

In Italy, if we felt like dessert we would step out and have some ice-cream or cake at the local **pasticceria**. If my mother prepared a dessert it meant that someone was invited over for dinner, and her dessert was always something that was great the next day (if we were fortunate enough to have some left over).

In summer, on the other hand, there was rarely a night that we did not have watermelon. We all knew summer was on its way when the watermelon stalls were set up by the local gypsies.

Dessert is very time-consuming and I never seem to have the time (or the skill) that it takes to make a great dessert. I have, however, served most of the dishes in this chapter at my restaurants over the years, to general acclaim. These recipes are some of my favourites and some of the easiest to make. Again, I want you to enjoy preparing and eating them. Some of the dishes are quintessentially Italian, such as tiramisù, and have always been part of my life.

# Tiramisù

Serves 6–8

1.2 litres short black coffee

800 ml water

500 ml marsala

300 ml kahlua

3 tablespoons coffee essence

1 tablespoon vanilla essence

1 kg savoiardi
(sponge finger) biscuits

200 g caster sugar

10 eggs, separated

1 kg mascarpone

200 g cocoa powder

This is a classic. Everyone's recipe is the best. I think this is a great one.

In a large bowl, combine coffee, water, marsala, kahlua, coffee essence and vanilla essence. Soak biscuits in this liquid for 1–2 minutes, or until they are completely wet.

In a bowl, beat sugar and egg yolks until fluffy, then fold into mascarpone. Separately, beat egg whites to form soft peaks, then fold into mascarpone mixture.

Place a layer of soaked biscuits on a baking tray. Spread some of the mascarpone mixture on top and dust generously with cocoa powder. Repeat process until all biscuits and mixture are used. Finish with a coating of cocoa powder. Refrigerate for 2 hours before serving.

Alternatively, to make individual tiramisù, follow the layering steps and repeat process in your favourite serving glass.

# Chocolate and amaretto zabaglione

Serves 4

500 g dark cooking chocolate

5 free-range egg yolks

250 g caster sugar

125 ml brandy

1.5 litres thickened cream

250 ml espresso

This is Robert Marchetti's Italian-style chocolate mousse.

Bring a saucepan of water to the boil, then reduce heat to a simmer. Break up chocolate and place in a bowl; sit bowl over water, ensuring that the bowl does not touch the water. Heat chocolate for 4 minutes, then turn heat off and leave chocolate to continue melting.

In a bowl, combine egg yolks, sugar and brandy. With a hand beater, whip ingredients until they are fluffy.

When chocolate is completely melted, remove bowl from water and set aside.

In a saucepan, heat egg mixture and beat with a whisk in a figure-of-eight shape for 6–8 minutes. (Keep heat low; heating the zabaglione mixture too intensely will turn it into scrambled eggs.) When mixture begins to coat the back of a spoon, remove from heat and allow to cool over a bowl of ice.

In a bowl, whip cream to form soft peaks. Stir espresso into chocolate. With a spatula, slowly mix zabaglione mixture into chocolate, then gently fold in cream. Spoon zabaglione into glasses or a large terrine dish, and chill for 1 hour before serving.

# Budino di riso

### INDIVIDUAL CHOCOLATE RICE PUDDINGS

Makes 4

150 g Arborio rice

700 ml milk

3 free-range eggs, separated

120 g caster sugar

180 g semi-sweet chocolate

80 g unsalted butter

2 tablespoons
caster sugar, extra

2 tablespoons finely
chopped dried figs

This is one of Robert Marchetti's sweet desserts.

Preheat oven to 200°C.

Bring a saucepan of lightly salted water to the boil, then add rice and boil for 10 minutes. Drain and return rice to pan. Add milk and cook over low heat, stirring constantly until all the milk is absorbed. Remove from heat.

In a bowl, beat egg yolks with sugar until fluffy. In a separate bowl, beat egg whites until stiff, gradually adding the extra sugar. In a small saucepan, melt chocolate and butter together.

In a large bowl, combine rice, egg yolk mixture, chocolate mixture, egg whites and figs by folding together gently with a spoon. Pour mixture into buttered and sugared dariole moulds, then cover with greased foil. Place moulds in a baking dish and fill dish with hot water to one-third of the way up the side of the moulds. Bake for 1 hour.

Remove moulds from water and place on a fresh and heated tray. Reduce oven temperature to 160°C. Return moulds to oven for a further 10 minutes. Remove from oven and leave to cool on a wire rack before removing puddings from moulds.

 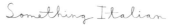

# Torta di nocciole e pere

HAZELNUT AND PEAR CAKE

Preheat oven to 180°C.

In a bowl, sift flour and cinnamon together, then add ground hazelnuts.

In a separate bowl, cream eggs and sugar. Add flour–cinnamon mixture and milk alternately to form a batter.

Core, peel and slice pears.

Grease a 30 cm springform tin and line with breadcrumbs. Pour half the batter into tin, then cover with half the sliced pears. Pour remaining batter over pears, then fan remaining pears to cover batter. Sprinkle chopped hazelnuts over pears and dot with butter. Bake for 1 hour, then remove from oven and cool, right-side up, on a wire rack. Store in an airtight container.

**350 g self-raising flour**

**1 teaspoon ground cinnamon**

**50 g ground hazelnuts**

**4 free-range eggs**

**400 g sugar**

**80 ml milk**

**50 g dry breadcrumbs**

**3 pears**

**50 g hazelnuts, roughly chopped**

**30 g butter**

# Biscotti alle mandorle

ALMOND BISCOTTI

Karen Martini created these sweet treats.

Preheat oven to 180°C.

In an electric mixer (or by hand), combine flour, baking powder and salt, then add butter and combine until powdery. Mix in sugar, ground almonds, coffee and cinnamon. Add eggs and mix briefly until a dough forms.

Turn dough out of electric mixer and finish mixing by hand. Shape dough into a rectangle, then cut into 3–4 cm bars and place on a baking tray. Bake for 25 minutes, then remove from oven and cool on a wire rack. Store biscotti in an airtight container.

Makes around
30 biscuits

**375 g plain flour**

**2 teaspoons baking powder**

**1 teaspoon salt**

**125 g unsalted butter, finely chopped**

**250 g caster sugar**

**180 g ground almonds**

**100 g freshly ground coffee**

**¼ teaspoon ground cinnamon**

**3 free-range eggs, lightly beaten**

# Choux puff crest with chocolate honey sauce and almond crème

This is one of Karen Martini's fabulous desserts.

### TO MAKE CHOUX PASTE

Preheat oven to 220°C.

In a saucepan, combine butter, milk, water, salt and sugar, and bring to the boil. Add flour, then beat mixture with a wooden spoon to combine. Reduce heat to medium and cook for 5 minutes, then remove from heat and place mixture in a food processor.

In a bowl, whisk eggs, then slowly add to food processor, allowing each addition to combine.

Sprinkle a baking tray with a little water. Place mixture into a piping bag fitted with a star nozzle and pipe doughnut-shaped rounds onto tray. Bake for 5 minutes, then open oven door and allow steam to escape. Reduce oven temperature to 180°C and bake for a further 10–15 minutes, to dry mixture out.

### TO MAKE ALMOND CRÈME

In a saucepan, heat milk, vanilla bean, lemon zest, butter, cream and 50 g of the sugar.

In a bowl, whisk remaining sugar into egg yolks, then whisk cornflour in, in 3 stages. Add heated milk mixture to yolk mixture, mixing well. Return mixture to pan and bring to a simmer, whisking constantly. Cook for 5 minutes, then reduce heat and add almond essence, stirring to mix. Remove from heat and pour mixture onto tray, and cover with plastic wrap.

### TO MAKE CHOCOLATE HONEY SAUCE

In a saucepan, melt chocolate, cream, honey and vanilla essence over low heat.

In a bowl, whisk cocoa powder into water. Add to chocolate mixture in pan. Stir until melted and almost simmering, then remove from heat and stir in butter, knob by knob. ➤

Serves 4–6

**250 ml pouring cream**

**icing sugar, for dusting**

choux paste

**80 g butter**

**100 ml milk**

**100 ml water**

**½ teaspoon salt**

**⅔ teaspoon sugar**

**120 g flour**

**3 large free-range eggs**

almond crème

**500 ml milk**

**½ vanilla bean**

**finely grated zest of ½ lemon**

**25 g butter**

**250 ml cream**

**100 g sugar**

**4 free-range egg yolks**

**50 g cornflour**

**1 drop almond essence**

chocolate honey sauce

**200 g dark chocolate**

**100 ml cream**

**60 g honey**

**1 teaspoon vanilla essence**

**3 tablespoons cocoa powder**

**75 ml water**

**25 g butter, roughly chopped** ➤

**praline almond**

**2 teaspoons grapeseed oil
(or any non-flavoured oil)**

**150 g sugar**

**250 g toasted almonds**

TO MAKE PRALINE ALMOND

Pour oil over a metal baking tray.

In a very clean saucepan (any impurities in the pan will make the sugar crystallise), moisten sugar with 2 teaspoons water, then bring to the boil. When sugar caramelises, add almonds and remove pan from heat. Pour mixture onto prepared tray and allow to cool.

When mixture is cool, place praline in silicon paper and smash with a rolling pin to crush almonds. Store praline in an airtight container.

TO SERVE

Cut choux crest in half and lay both halves flat, centre up, on a serving plate.

In the bowl of an electric mixer, beat 1 cup of the almond crème with pouring cream until smooth. Place mixture into a piping bag fitted with a star nozzle. Fill base of each crest with almond crème, then top with lid.

Pour chocolate honey sauce over the top, and allow to pool on plate. Sprinkle choux crests with praline almond and dust with icing sugar to serve.

# Gelato affogato

DROWNED ICE-CREAM

Serves 4

**8 scoops premium
vanilla ice-cream**

**2 cups freshly made espresso**

**200 ml tiramisù liqueur**

**2 teaspoons freshly
ground coffee**

This dessert has been served in every business I have owned. It has many versions, and this is my favourite.

In serving bowls, place 2 scoops of ice-cream per person. Pour ½ cup hot espresso over each scoop, then pour 50 ml of tiramisù liqueur over each scoop. Sprinkle each scoop with ½ teaspoon ground coffee and serve.

*Gelato affogato*

# Raspberry and Chianti sorbet

Serves 8

**350 g caster sugar**

**750 ml Chianti wine**

**finely grated zest of 1 lemon**

**6 sprigs fresh mint**

**500 g fresh raspberries**

To make this dish, by Robert Marchetti, you need an ice-cream machine. Only use good-quality Chianti.

In a saucepan, combine sugar, wine, lemon zest and mint over high heat. Bring to the boil, then reduce heat and simmer for 2 minutes. Remove from heat, add raspberries and set aside for 1 hour.

Remove and discard mint and lemon zest. Remove raspberries from cooking liquid (reserving cooking liquid) and push through a fine-mesh strainer into liquid – don't leave anything behind but seeds. Add half the seeds to raspberry purée.

Add purée to ice-cream machine and set aside until semi-set. Transfer mixture to a large bowl and allow to set in freezer for 3 hours.

To serve, spoon sorbet into a piping bag and pipe into glasses. Serve with chocolate sponge finger biscuits or any other favourites.

# Rhubarb and polenta cake

Serves 8–10

½ fresh rhubarb stem
650 g caster sugar
450 g softened
unsalted butter
450 g ground almonds
2 teaspoons vanilla essence
6 whole free-range eggs
grated zest of 4 lemons
juice of 1 lemon
1½ teaspoons baking powder
225 g polenta flour
¼ teaspoon salt

In a saucepan, heat rhubarb and 100 g of the sugar over low heat. Simmer for 4–5 minutes to soften (do not stir, otherwise the rhubarb may lose its shape), then remove from heat and strain, retaining liquid. Set sugared rhubarb aside in colander, and liquid in a bowl, for 1 hour.

Preheat oven 160°C.

Butter and flour a 30 cm round baking tin, then line it with baking paper, pressing down to expel air. (Do not use a springform baking tin, otherwise the rhubarb will leak through as it is cooking.) Spoon cooled rhubarb onto base of tin.

Place butter in the bowl of an electric mixer. Add the remaining sugar and beat until pale, then fold in ground almonds and vanilla essence. Continue beating and add eggs one at a time. Fold in lemon zest, lemon juice, baking powder, polenta flour and salt.

Carefully spoon cake mix over rhubarb (take care not to squash the rhubarb). Bake for 45–50 minutes. (To test cake, insert a skewer in centre – if it comes out clean, the cake is cooked.) Remove from oven and allow to cool in tin for 1 hour, then turn cake out onto a wire rack to cool completely. Serve with yoghurt and the rhubarb juices.

# Torta di limone e ricotta

LEMON AND RICOTTA TART

Preheat oven to 170°C.

In a cake tin, lay a baking sheet and add pastry. Bake for 20–25 minutes, or until golden brown and crispy. Remove from oven and set aside.

Place ricotta and cream in the bowl of an electric mixer. Purée until smooth, then add mascarpone and blend. Add lemon juice and zest. Add eggs one at a time, then add sugar. Mix thoroughly, then pour mixture over pastry case and bake for 30–40 minutes, or until mixture is set. Allow tart to cool, then serve with cream.

**pastry**

**400 g quick puff pastry (see recipe on page 152)**

**filling**

**750 g fresh ricotta**

**2 cups cream**

**2 kg mascarpone**

**juice and finely grated zest of 10–12 lemons**

**8 free-range eggs**

**450 g sugar**

lemons

Vanilla pannacotta

# Vanilla pannacotta

Pannacotta is the dish to judge an Italian restaurant by. The texture is important.

In a large bowl, soak gelatine in milk to soften.

In a saucepan, combine 500 ml of the cream with sugar, vanilla bean and lemon rind. Bring to the boil, then remove pan from heat. Strain mixture into gelatine mixture and stir to dissolve gelatine. Add alcohol if desired. Cool to room temperature.

Whip remaining cream until soft peaks form, then gently fold into cooled gelatine mixture. Pour into moulds and refrigerate for a minimum of 3–5 hours.

To serve, dip base of each mould in warm water to release pannacotta from mould. Serve with poached fruit and crostoli (see recipe on page 150).

(see recipe on page 150)

Serves 6–8

**4 gelatine leaves**

**300 ml cold milk**

**900 ml pouring cream (35 per cent butter fat)**

**120 g caster sugar**

**1 vanilla bean, split lengthways**

**finely grated zest of 1 lemon (preferably unwaxed)**

**120 ml alcohol of your choice (optional)**

# Torta di cioccolato

## QUICK CHOCOLATE CAKE

I am impatient with making desserts, so this recipe, created by Robert Marchetti, is for those of you who are the same.

Preheat oven to 180°C. Butter a 30 cm round cake tin.

In a food processor, mix butter, chocolate and coffee. Add sugar, flour and cocoa powder and mix again. Add eggs and vanilla, then mix and pour into cake tin. Bake for 45 minutes. (To test cake, insert a skewer in centre – if it comes out clean, the cake is cooked.) Remove from oven and allow to cool in tin for 1 hour then turn cake out onto a wire rack to cool completely. Serve with cream.

Serves 6–8

**250 g softened butter**

**250 g dark chocolate, chopped**

**250 ml strong coffee**

**200 g caster sugar**

**200 g self-raising flour**

**50 g cocoa powder**

**2 free-range eggs**

**2 teaspoons vanilla essence**

# Crostoli

CRISP SWEET PASTRIES

**Makes 20–30 pieces**

325 g plain flour

250 g self-raising flour

4 free-range eggs

3 tablespoons caster sugar

300 ml sweet sherry

juice of ½ lemon

2 tablespoons unsalted butter

3 litres cottonseed oil,
for frying

icing sugar, to serve

Crostoli require patience to make. My family often had these on the table during festive periods.

In a bowl, combine flours and make a well in the centre.

In a separate bowl, beat eggs with sugar, sherry and lemon juice. Pour mixture into centre of flour and mix with a fork. Soften butter then slowly add to form a smooth dough (the dough should not be too wet). Set dough aside for 30 minutes.

Roll dough to sheets 5 mm thick, then cut into shapes around 1.5 cm × 13 cm. Slice two parallel slits from one end to the other, but stop short about 1 cm from each end. Plait the dough like a bow.

In a heavy saucepan or deep fryer, heat oil to 160°C (to test, use a thermometer, or drop a piece of pastry into the oil; it should sizzle immediately). Fry crostoli a few at a time until golden brown on both sides. (Make sure you don't overcrowd the pan, otherwise the crostoli will not crisp evenly.) Lay hot crostoli on absorbent paper to remove any excess oil. When crostoli are cooled, sprinkle with icing sugar to serve.

Crostoli will last for many weeks sealed in an airtight container and stored in a dark room.

# Moscato d'Asti pannacotta

**Serves 6–8**

**700 ml *moscato d'Asti* wine**

**80 g sugar**

**200 ml milk**

**500 ml cream**

**3 gelatine leaves**

**2 teaspoons orange blossom water**

Karen Martini created this sweet dessert.

In a saucepan, heat 500 ml of the *moscato d'Asti* wine over medium heat. Simmer until liquid has reduced to 100 ml.

In a separate saucepan, heat the remaining wine until almost simmering, then add sugar. Separately, heat milk and cream together, then add to wine mix and heat until simmering. Remove from heat and cool for 10 minutes.

Lay gelatine leaves in cold water to soften for 2–4 minutes.

Add reduced wine to milk–wine mixture, then add orange blossom water and gelatine leaves. Mix well and strain. Ladle into dishes (or your preferred style of mould, around 100 ml in volume), wrap individually in plastic and set in refrigerator.

To serve, dip base of each mould in warm water to release pannacotta from mould.

# Pasta sfoglia

QUICK PUFF PASTRY

**Makes 1.5 kg**

**1 kg plain flour**

**1 teaspoon salt**

**800 g chilled butter, cut into 2 cm cubes**

**450 ml water**

**squeeze of lemon**

Sift flour onto a workbench then sprinkle with salt. Mix butter cubes evenly through flour with fingertips, then gradually incorporate water and lemon juice, mixing lightly to form a rough dough. Shape dough into a rectangle and roll to 3 times the original length. Fold dough in thirds, one end over the other (like a letter). Turn dough so the open end faces you, and roll and fold as before. Wrap and refrigerate for 30 minutes. Repeat process twice, resting dough before rolling each time.

Cut into thirds and store, layering between sheets of plastic and enclosed in a plastic bag, for 3–4 days in the refrigerator.

# Toasted nut cassata

Line a 25 cm springform tin with foil.

Roughly chop cherries and place in a bowl. Cover with brandy and allow to stand for 10 minutes.

Whip cream and sugar until stiff, then fold in cherries and brandy (be careful not to knock out too much air). Spoon cream mixture into springform tin, spread evenly and freeze.

In a saucepan, melt chocolate over low heat. Divide ice-cream in half. Add half of the first batch of divided ice-cream to the chocolate to begin the mixing process. Add remaining half of the first batch of ice-cream, and mix. Mix the remaining batch of ice-cream into the chocolate mix and evenly spread over the frozen cream inside the cake tin.

In a bowl, crumble biscuits and almonds together roughly. Set aside.

Once the cassata has set, turn it out onto a bench and sprinkle nut mixture on top. With a thin-blade knife, cut into thick slices to serve.

Serves 4–6

**300 g glacé cherries**

**2 tablespoons brandy**

**300 ml thickened cream**

**2 tablespoons caster sugar**

**125 g dark chocolate**

**2 litres good-quality vanilla ice-cream**

**60 g coconut biscuits**

**60 g flaked almonds**

cherries

Mezzanotte

This is my favourite style of eating, and late at night is usually when I have time to eat. When I come home from the restaurant it's usually around one o'clock in the morning and I want to eat something quick, easy and tasty. I might invite a few friends from work over, and we will open a bottle of wine and sit around until the early hours of the morning; naturally, we get hungry, and these recipes are perfect for this kind of snack. You can of course prepare these snacks at any time of the day, but they are wonderfully suited to an after-dinner appetite.

A lot of these recipes come from our bar menu at Icebergs and The Melbourne Wine Room. We have clients come in for a drink, and they might have a couple of bottles of wine or a few spirits and start to get hungry, so we give them some snacks to eat as they drink and chat.

# Parmesan, grissini and olives

Serves 4

500 g pizza flour (or strong bakers' flour)

1 teaspoon sea salt

325 ml warm water

3 teaspoons dry yeast

60 ml olive oil

extra-virgin olive oil, for drizzling

sea salt, extra

20 large olives

500 g fresh parmesan

This dish is a great starter or antipasto and arose from my early days at Caffé e Cucina. This dish was voted by Melbourne food critic Rita Erlich as one of her top 10 favourite dishes; it has since been on all of my menus in some variation.

In a large bowl, sift flour and salt together, and make a well in the centre.

In a separate bowl, whisk warm water, yeast and oil together, then pour into flour well. Use your hands to mix ingredients into a wet, sticky dough. Turn dough out onto a floured bench and knead for 10–15 minutes, adding more flour if needed. Return dough to bowl, cover with a clean tea towel and set aside in a warm place to prove (rise) for 20–40 minutes, or until dough has doubled in size.

Preheat oven to 160°C.

Break dough into walnut-sized pieces. Sprinkle bench with extra pizza flour. Using your hands, roll dough pieces into thin 30 cm sticks. (Mixture will make about 25 sticks.)

Lightly oil a heavy-duty baking tray and place bread sticks upon it, spaced slightly apart. Bake for 15–20 minutes, or until crisp. Remove from oven, drizzle with extra-virgin oil over and season well with salt while still hot. Leave to cool.

Serve with olives and broken chunks of parmesan.

*Carpaccio ripieno di mascarpone*

# Carpaccio ripieno di mascarpone

CARPACCIO OF BEEF FILLED WITH MASCARPONE

This is a great canapé or snack.

Roll some long, thin slices of top-quality raw beef with salt, pepper, lemon juice and mascarpone. Serve with lemon wedges and a green salad. It's that simple.

# Spaghetti con burro

SPAGHETTI WITH BUTTER

I make this for my son, Sylvester, when I have been very disorganised and not planned ahead. It is also the perfect dish late at night. Make sure the butter is straight from the fridge – if it is too soft it will split, lose its creaminess and become oily.

Bring a saucepan of well-salted water to the boil and add spaghetti. While spaghetti is cooking, cut butter into bite-sized cubes, place in a bowl and season with salt and pepper. When spaghetti is al dente, add to bowl and mix

Serves 2

**300 g spaghetti**

**200 g unsalted cultured butter**

**sea salt and freshly ground black pepper**

**200 g freshly grated parmesan**

# Olive al forno

**100 ml olive oil**

**500 g black or green olives**

**4 bay leaves**

**6 cloves garlic**

**200 ml dry white wine**

**freshly ground black pepper**

This is the perfect tempter and a great bar snack: five minutes' preparation, a glass of wine, and your appetite is sharpened.

Preheat oven to 180°C.

Heat oil in a heavy-based frying pan over medium heat, then add olives, bay leaves and garlic and cook until olives begin to spit. Add wine and remove pan from heat. Transfer olives to a baking tray and bake for 4–5 minutes, or until heated through. Season with pepper and serve with grissini (see recipe on page 181) or crusty bread.

# Prosciutto e pere

PROSCIUTTO WITH SLICED PEAR

Serves 4

**100 ml extra-virgin olive oil**

**4 ripe brown-skinned pears, sliced**

**100 ml aged balsamic vinegar**

**12 very thin slices prosciutto**

**15 grissini sticks (see recipe on page 181)**

**½ lemon, cut into wedges**

In a bowl, mix oil, pears and balsamic vinegar.

Lay prosciutto flat on a serving platter, then spoon pear mixture on top. Serve with grissini (see recipe on page 181) and lemon wedges.

*Olive al forno*

# Prosciutto e melone all'agro dolce

PROSCIUTTO WITH SWEET AND SOUR MELON

Serves 4

1 large rockmelon

100 ml aged balsamic vinegar

sea salt and freshly ground
black pepper

extra-virgin olive oil, to taste

16 very thin slices prosciutto

handful rocket

2 lemons, sliced

This is a very '90s dish, but it's still a favourite of mine. Its Southern Italian influences made it a favourite at Caffé e Cucina during our early years. A little chilli is a great addition in summer.

With a melon-baller, ball rockmelon flesh into a bowl. Add balsamic vinegar, salt, pepper and a drizzle of extra-virgin olive oil. Lay 4 slices of prosciutto each on 4 plates. Spoon melon mixture over prosciutto, then sprinkle with a few rocket leaves and lemon slices.

# Pinzimonio

RAW VEGETABLES WITH CONDIMENTS

Serves 4

4 baby zucchini

2 baby cucumbers

2 mild red chillies

2 baby bell peppers

5 yellow cherry tomatoes

5 red cherry tomatoes

1 head treviso

1 head baby fennel

1 small bunch baby
pearl onions

1 bunch white or green
young asparagus

5 fresh Borlotti beans

2 radishes

3 baby carrots

2 baby zucchini flowers

This dish is all about fresh, great-tasting vegetables. It's perfect for a summer's night and is great with *salsa verde* (see recipe on page 169) and balsamic mayonnaise (see recipe on page 168).

Chop all vegetables into desired sizes, then toss them in a bowl, add lemon juice and mix well.

Fill a deep platter with crushed ice. Separate vegetables and place each vegetable over ice. Serve vegetables chilled.

*Pinzimonio*

# Stracchino con cotogna

Serves 4

500 g stracchino cheese

100 g quince paste

50 ml extra-virgin olive oil

freshly ground black pepper

handful rocket

½ lemon

Stracchino is a great cheese. Serve it with a bottle of young, chilled Verdicchio Italian white. This dish is often referred to as the 'Romeo and Juliet' because it is very popular in Verona.

Slice stracchino into 4 wedges. Arrange cheese and quince paste on a serving plate, then drizzle with extra-virgin olive oil and season with pepper. Arrange rocket on plate and finish with a squeeze of lemon.

# Spaghetti aglio con olio e pangrattato

SPAGHETTI WITH GARLIC, CHILLI AND BREADCRUMBS

Serves 4

500 g spaghetti

300 ml olive oil

6 cloves garlic, finely chopped

4 small red chillies, deseeded and thinly sliced

200 g fresh breadcrumbs

sea salt and freshly ground black pepper

½ bunch parsley, leaves picked

400 g grated fresh parmesan

juice of 1 lemon

A late-night classic for anyone with an empty cupboard.

Bring a saucepan of well-salted water to the boil and add spaghetti. When spaghetti is 4–5 minutes away from al dente, heat 100 ml of the oil in a frying pan over low heat. Add garlic and chilli and fry gently for 2–3 minutes, or until garlic is light brown, then add breadcrumbs. Fry for a further 2 minutes, then season with salt and pepper. Add remaining oil and the parsley. When spaghetti is al dente, add to pan and mix well. Drizzle lemon juice over and serve with parmesan.

# Parmigiano con miele

PARMESAN WITH HONEY

This is the perfect way to finish a hard day and to impress friends.
It's a good idea to always have some parmesan in your fridge.

Break parmesan into large bite-sized chunks and arrange on a serving plate
with walnuts. Drizzle honey over, and serve.

**300 g fresh parmesan
(Parmigiano-Reggiano is ideal)**

**300 g freshly shelled walnuts**

**truffle honey (or good
meadow honey), for drizzling**

walnuts

Ricette Semplici

# RICETTE SEMPLICI

*These recipes are very basic and will complement many meals. These are some of the staples, the must-haves, the things I cannot do without. From the most basic necessities – pasta dough, stocks and pasta sauces – to wonderful side dishes – potato mash, polenta and pesto – most of these dishes can be prepared with little effort and do not require much culinary knowledge. The side dishes are the most popular that we have served. The salads require very basic, fresh ingredients, and remain true to my philosophy of having the courage to keep things simple.*

# Basic pasta dough

Makes 450 g

**300 g plain flour**
**3 large free-range eggs**
**pinch of salt**

Place flour on a firm, cold surface and make a well in the centre.

In a bowl, whisk eggs and salt together, and pour into centre of flour well. With a fork, stir eggs into flour until mixed, then fold gently with your hands until mixture forms a coarse dough.

Wash and dry your hands, then lightly flour your work surface and knead dough with the heel of your hands, pushing it gently away and pulling it back. Continue kneading for 10–15 minutes, or until dough is durable and elastic. Allow dough to rest for 30 minutes before using.

When making filled pasta, do not let the dough dry out too much. For filled pasta, roll dough to around 2 mm thickness; for other styles, such as lasagna, roll to around 4 mm thickness.

# Balsamic mayonnaise

Makes 300 g

**3 free-range egg yolks**
**260 ml extra-virgin olive oil**
**juice of ½ lemon**
**50 ml balsamic vinegar**
**sea salt and freshly ground black pepper**

In a large bowl, mix egg yolks together with a whisk. Continue whisking and slowly drizzle in oil until mixture is thick and all oil is added. (If mixture splits – this can happen if the oil is poured too quickly – add a little warm water and another broken yolk, and repeat process.) Add lemon juice and vinegar, and season with salt and pepper.

# Salsa verde

This is a cold sauce to be eaten with simple grilled meats, fish or even raw vegetables.

Place potatoes in a saucepan of cold water. Bring water to the boil and cook potatoes for 6–8 minutes, or until tender, then drain and set aside to cool. When cooled, cut into 1 cm cubes.

In a bowl, combine red-wine vinegar and sherry vinegar, then add potato cubes. Cut bread into 1 cm cubes and add to bowl. Mix well and set aside to soak for 20 minutes.

Meanwhile, in a separate bowl, combine all remaining ingredients and mix well. (If *salsa verde* is too dry, add a little extra-virgin olive oil.)

Combine all ingredients and mix well.

The *salsa verde* will keep for 4–6 hours before starting to change colour.

*basil*

**Serves 4–6**

**3 large kipfler potatoes, peeled**

**100 ml aged red-wine vinegar**

**100 ml sherry vinegar**

**2 handfuls day-old sourdough bread**

**2 bunches flat-leaf parsley, stalks removed and leaves roughly chopped**

**½ bunch basil, stalks removed and leaves roughly chopped**

**1 bunch chives, roughly chopped**

**½ bunch mint, stalks removed and leaves roughly chopped**

**300 ml extra-virgin olive oil**

**freshly ground black pepper**

**1 small Spanish onion, peeled and finely chopped**

**6 baby gherkins, finely chopped**

**250 g pickled vegetables (available at Italian delicatessens), finely chopped**

**2 cloves garlic, finely chopped**

**100 g marinated anchovies, finely chopped**

*Insalata di broccolini e pomodoro*

# Radicchio alla griglia e funghi alla griglia

GRILLED RADICCHIO AND GRILLED MUSHROOMS

This dish is great when cooked on a barbecue, and it is excellent as a side for sausages.

Rub extra-virgin olive oil into some fresh radicchio wedges, then rub in some crushed garlic. Barbecue until radicchio wedges are soft and then finish with some lemon juice. To make *funghi alla griglia*, follow the same steps but substitute field mushrooms for radicchio wedges.

# Insalata di broccolini e pomodoro

SALAD OF BROCCOLINI AND TOMATO

In a bowl, squash tomatoes with your hands to extract juice. Season with salt and pepper, then add lemon juice, oregano and oil. Mix well and set aside.

Bring a saucepan of well salted water to the boil. Add broccolini and cook for 3–4 minutes, or until firm but tender. Drain and add to tomato bowl straight away (do not allow broccolini to cool). Add vinegar and refrigerate for 10 minutes.

Meanwhile, tear bread into bite-sized pieces.

Remove from refrigerator and add bread, parsley and basil, and check seasoning.

**Serves 2**

**2 soft, ripe tomatoes, roughly chopped**

**sea salt and freshly ground black pepper**

**juice of 1 lemon**

**10 leaves oregano, finely chopped**

**200 ml extra-virgin olive oil**

**1 bunch broccolini**

**2 tablespoons red-wine vinegar**

**200 g day-old sourdough bread**

**¼ bunch flat-leaf parsley, roughly chopped**

**6 basil leaves**

# Insalata di fichi e rucola

## SALAD OF FIG AND ROCKET

**100 ml milk**

**2 cloves garlic, peeled**

**50 ml olive oil**

**4 figs, sliced into 1 cm discs**

**2 tablespoons extra-virgin olive oil**

**handful rocket**

**100 ml apple balsamic vinegar**

**1 tablespoon red-wine vinegar**

**100 g shaved fresh parmesan**

**juice of 1 lemon**

**sea salt and freshly ground black pepper**

**lemon wedges, to serve**

Heat a small saucepan over high heat and add milk and garlic. Bring to the boil, then turn heat off. Strain and discard milk, and return garlic to pan. Add enough water to almost fill pan and return to heat. Bring to the boil, then turn heat off. Strain water and set garlic aside to cool. (Blanching the garlic in this way removes its heat and ensures that it doesn't overpower the salad.) When cool, slice garlics thinly.

Heat olive oil in a frying pan over low heat. Add garlic and fry until just brown, then remove and place garlic on absorbent paper to drain and cool.

Scatter figs over a serving plate.

In a bowl, combine extra-virgin olive oil, rocket, apple balsamic, red-wine vinegar, parmesan and lemon juice, and season with salt and pepper. Mix well and scatter mixture over figs. Finish by sprinkling garlic over salad, and serve with lemon wedges.

# Pickled radicchio

**Serves 4**

**1 litre vegetable oil**

**300 ml balsamic vinegar**

**5 radicchio hearts, washed**

**sea salt and freshly ground black pepper**

**extra-virgin olive oil**

This dish of Robert Marchetti's makes a great antipasto, or you can serve it with some grilled beef or duck.

In a deep, heavy-based frying pan, bring vegetable oil and vinegar to the boil. Add radicchio hearts and remove pan from heat. Season with salt and pepper, then remove radicchios from liquid as soon as they have cooked (take care to not undercook or overcook the radicchios; they should be tender and not bitter). Transfer radicchio hearts to a metal bowl and allow to cool. Marinate with enough extra-virgin olive oil to just cover.

You can store the radicchio hearts in a sealed, sterilised container at room temperature for 4–6 weeks.

*Insalata di fichi e rucola*

# Basil pesto

Serves 4–6

**5 cloves garlic, peeled**

**200 g pine nuts**

**100 ml extra-virgin olive oil**

**sea salt and freshly ground black pepper**

**3 handfuls basil leaves**

**300 g grated fresh parmesan**

This is Robert Marchetti's version of a classic pesto.

In the bowl of an electric mixer, combine garlic, pine nuts and 100 ml of the oil. Mix for 5–6 minutes, or until a paste forms, then season with salt and pepper. (Add minimal salt, because parmesan is quite salty.) Continue mixing on a slow speed and add basil leaves a handful at time until you have a smooth paste. (If paste becomes dry, add a little extra-virgin olive oil, but take care not to add too much, otherwise the mixture will separate.) Add parmesan and the remaining oil, and continue to mix on a slow speed for 30 seconds. (Take care not to over-mix, otherwise the basil will blacken.) Adjust seasoning if required.

You can store pesto in a sealed jar (cover top of pesto with extra-virgin olive oil) in the fridge for 2–3 weeks.

# Salsa di pomodoro

## TOMATO SALSA

Serves 8–10 as a side dish

**20 Roma tomatoes, finely chopped**

**4 cloves garlic, finely chopped**

**½ bunch basil, torn**

**500 ml extra-virgin olive oil**

**juice of 2 lemons**

**sea salt and freshly ground black pepper**

This salsa is wonderful with grilled bread, or tossed through pasta. If you want to make this dish for fewer people, simply halve the ingredients.

In a bowl, mix tomato, garlic, basil, oil and lemon juice together, then season well with salt and pepper.

# Polenta

Robert Marchetti's polenta goes wonderfully well with rocket and a little chilli as a great starter, or as a side dish to meat or a casserole.

In a saucepan, bring the water to the boil. Slowly whisk in polenta and oil, and season with salt and pepper. Cook polenta as per instructions on the packet (or until no longer sandy). Fold both cheeses and butter through polenta. On a baking tray, spread mixture to 2 cm thickness and allow to set before serving.

Serves 4–6

4.5 litres water

1 kg polenta

125 ml olive oil

sea salt and freshly ground black pepper

200 g grated fresh parmesan

500 g fontina cheese, grated

200 g butter

# Potato mash

In a large, deep saucepan, bring plenty of water to a low boil and add potatoes. Slowly boil for 1½ hours, or until just soft (take care not to overcook). Drain potatoes, then transfer to a large bowl and mash until smooth.

In a small saucepan, bring cream and butter to the boil. While potatoes are still hot, pour hot cream mixture over and whisk vigorously until well combined and smooth. Season with salt.

Serves 2–4

2.5 kg Desiree potatoes, peeled

500 ml cream
(35 per cent butter fat)

150 g unsalted butter

sea salt

# Lemon vinaigrette

In a bowl, crush garlic with salt, then add mustard and mix to form a paste. Add vinegar and lemon juice, then the oils. (Do not overmix.)

Makes 6 cups
(and some for the fridge)

3 cloves garlic

2 tablespoons salt

2 tablespoons Dijon mustard

125 ml red-wine vinegar

125 ml lemon juice

500 ml olive oil

500 ml extra-virgin olive oil

# Insalata di finocchio e rucola

## SALAD OF FENNEL AND ROCKET

**Serves 2**

1 tablespoon fennel seeds

2 bulbs baby fennel

juice of 1 lemon

150 ml virgin olive oil

1 clove garlic, finely chopped

50 ml white-wine vinegar

4 basil leaves, torn

6 mint leaves, torn

1 lemon, peeled and divided into 6 segments

2 handfuls rocket

sea salt and freshly ground black pepper

This is a very crisp summer salad that makes a great starter or accompaniment to fish.

Heat a frying pan over low heat and add fennel seeds. With a spoon, constantly move seeds around pan for 2–3 minutes. Remove seeds from pan and set aside on a plate to cool. When cool, use a mortar and pestle to pound seeds to a fine powder. (If you do not have a mortar and pestle, place seeds in a clean tea towel and bash with a meat tenderiser.) Set aside.

Slice fennel bulbs in half and remove stalk from middle. Remove tops from fennel, then cut fennel into 5 mm slices.

In a mixing bowl, combine all ingredients and season with salt and pepper.

# Spinaci saltati

## SAUTÉED SPINACH

**Serves 4**

2 kg baby spinach, washed

150 ml olive oil

3 cloves garlic, crushed

sea salt and freshly ground black pepper

2 lemons

This is the most popular side dish I have ever served.

Bring a saucepan of salted water to the boil, then add spinach and boil for 5 minutes, or until tender. Drain and squeeze spinach by hand to remove excess water.

Heat a heavy-based frying pan over low heat and add oil and garlic. Fry slowly (do not allow garlic to brown) until garlic is soft, then add spinach and fry slowly until all water has evaporated. Remove from pan and season with salt and pepper. Serve with a squeeze of lemon with some wedges on the side.

*Insalata di finocchio e rucola*

*Insalata Caprese*

# Insalata Caprese

I love this version of the *insalata Caprese*. Robert Marchetti has added his special touch.

With a fork, spike chillies all over (this will ensure they don't explode when cooked). Turn a gas burner on your stove onto high. Using tongs, hold chillies directly over flame and cook until black and blistered. Remove from heat and set aside to cool for 2–3 minutes. Cut chillies in half lengthways and remove seeds. Cut lengthways again, into strips.

Slice tomatoes into ½ cm discs and arrange on a serving plate.

In a bowl, combine yoghurt, lemon juice, oregano, vinegar, oil, basil and mozzarella, and season with salt and pepper. Arrange mixture over tomato and scatter chilli over the top.

**Serves 2**

**2 long red chillies**

**2 ripe tomatoes**

**100 ml sheep's yoghurt**

**juice of 1 lemon**

**8 oregano leaves**

**2 teaspoons white-wine vinegar**

**100 ml extra-virgin olive oil**

**10 basil leaves**

**4 pieces buffalo mozzarella, torn into bite-sized pieces**

**sea salt and freshly ground black pepper**

# Insalata di rucola con limone

I cannot get through my day without this dish. It is filled with the flavours of peasant Italy.

In a bowl, combine parmesan, oil, vinegar and lemon juice. Whisk until well mixed, and season with salt and pepper. Add rocket and parsley and mix well. Serve with lemon wedges.

**Serves 2**

**50 g grated fresh parmesan**

**150 ml extra-virgin olive oil**

**10 ml white-wine vinegar**

**juice of 1 lemon**

**sea salt and freshly ground black pepper**

**2 handfuls rocket**

**¼ bunch parsley, leaves picked**

**1 lemon, cut into wedges**

# Fish stock

Makes 2–3 litres

bones of 2½ barramundi (ask
your fishmonger for these)

100 ml olive oil

1½ carrots, finely chopped

¼ bulb fennel, finely chopped

1 onion, finely chopped

1½ sticks celery, finely
chopped

½ head garlic, halved

1 bay leaf

½ bunch parsley stalks

5 peppercorns

1½ sprigs thyme

finely grated zest of
½ lemon

750 ml white wine

This stock recipe (and the chicken stock below) of Robert Marchetti's is a staple for your kitchen.

Wash fish bones twice in cold water. Remove and discard gills and entrails.

Heat oil in a large, deep saucepan over medium heat and add carrot, fennel, onion, celery, garlic, bay leaf, parsley, peppercorns, thyme and lemon zest. Cook gently until vegetables have softened (do not allow to brown), then add wine. Reduce heat and simmer for 4–5 minutes, or until liquid has reduced by two-thirds. Add fish bones and cook for 5 minutes. Add enough cold water to cover up to 10 cm above bones, then bring to the boil, skimming frequently to remove impurities that rise to the top. Reduce heat and simmer for 20 minutes, skimming. Remove stock from heat and allow it to sit for 20 minutes. Strain stock through a sieve to remove remaining impurities.

# Chicken stock

Makes 5 litres

5 kg chicken bones

2 chicken wings

1 carrot, chopped

1 stick celery, chopped

1 head garlic, halved

1 large onion, chopped

1 sprig thyme

4 peppercorns

1 bay leaf

1 bunch parsley stalks

Place chicken bones and wings in a large, deep saucepan and cover with cold water. Bring to the boil, skimming frequently to remove impurities that rise to the top. Add remaining ingredients and bring back to the boil. Skim again. Reduce heat and simmer for 4 hours.

# Grissini

BREAD STICKS

These bread sticks are the perfect accompaniment.

In a bowl, sift 250 g of the flour with a pinch of salt and make a well in the centre.

In a separate bowl, combine warm water, yeast and the 2 tablespoons of olive oil. Mix well and pour into flour well, stirring with a wooden spoon until well mixed and sticky.

Dust bench with the remaining flour, then transfer dough to a workbench. With your hands, knead dough for 12–15 minutes, or until it is durable and elastic. Pour 20 ml olive oil into a bowl and place dough on top. Pour remaining olive oil over top of dough and cover with a clean tea towel. Leave dough in a warm place to prove (rise) for 1 hour, or until it has doubled in size.

Preheat oven to 150°C.

Transfer dough to bench and knead back to its original size. Cut into 30 bite-sized pieces. With the palm of your hand, roll dough balls forwards and backwards until you have long, thin strips the thickness of a straw. Continue process until all dough is rolled into strips.

Lightly sprinkle a baking tray with semolina and lay grissini sticks on tray. Bake for 15 minutes, or until crisp and crunchy. (If grissini slightly bend, bake for an extra 5 minutes.) Remove from oven and season with generous amounts of salt and pepper, and drizzle with extra-virgin olive oil. Return grissini to oven and bake for a further 5 minutes.

You can store grissini in an airtight container for up to 2 days.

Makes 30
grissini sticks

**550 g pizza flour (or strong bakers' flour), for dough**

**sea salt**

**325 ml lukewarm water**

**½ × 7 g packet of dry yeast**

**40 ml olive oil**

**2 tablespoons olive oil**

**300 g fine semolina**

**freshly ground black pepper**

**extra-virgin olive oil, for drizzling**

# Something Personal

There are so many people to thank, but first and most importantly I must thank all my clients for their continued support over the past sixteen years, in particular those who have become good friends. Thank you, Dino and Josh.

I would like to thank all the waiters of the world because we all know your product is as good as the way in which you serve it.

A very special thank you to my current business partners, Micheal Supuntasis, Karen Martini, Anthony De Thomasis, Marino Angelini, Mario Venneri, Tony Zaccagnini, Terry Burke and Antonio Massaria. I hope we can continue to do business together for a long time. A special thank you to Mario for continuing to believe in me.

A very special thank you also to all current owners of businesses I have been involved in – Caffé e Cucina: Authur Georgiou; Il Bàcaro: Joe Mamone; Café Veloce: Peter Van Haandel and Mike Benko; Otto Ristorante and Nove Pizzeria: John Laws and Lang Walker – for maintaining and improving these businesses.

This book would not have been possible without the assistance of Robert Marchetti and Karen Martini. Thank you, Robert, for making these recipes possible. Thank you for teaching me so much – I only wish we had worked together years ago. Thank you, Karen, for your inspiration. As my mother always said: 'Food I would never cook but flavours I recognise.'

To all the people I have worked with, thank you for being understanding of my demands. David, Fiona, Chris, Tony, Thomas, Carl, Sandra and Claudio: you have always produced beautiful work.

A special thank you to Chris Connell for allowing us to use your archives.

A very special thank you to David Band for your wonderful illustrations.

David Matheson, it was a real pleasure to work with you. I know you are as proud as I am of what we achieved.

Julie Gibbs, thank you for your patience, incredible support and honesty.

Thank you, Bill Tikos (from Diversity Management), for making this book possible.

Claire de Medici, we could not have survived without you.

Deborah Brash, thank you for your vision.

To everyone else at Penguin Books: SORRY! But let's celebrate and have a glass of champagne. I can work a hundred hours on the floor every week without fail but I never seemed to find the time to write this book.

To all my suppliers over the years, all I can say is *grazie*.

Rochelle Ward, thank you for being a great mother and for looking after Sylvester the endless nights that I worked.

Maria Farmer, once again I must thank you for steering me in the right direction. I wonder how I survived without you.

Sneaky Sound System, your music is a joy.

To Kirrily, my best friend and partner, thank you for being part of my life. Thank you for your creativity, dedication and love.

# Index

Entries in *italics* indicate photographs.

LANTERN

Published by the Penguin Group
Penguin Group (Australia)
250 Camberwell Road, Camberwell, Victoria 3124, Australia
(a division of Pearson Australia Group Pty Ltd)
Penguin Group (USA) Inc.
375 Hudson Street, New York, New York 10014, USA
Penguin Group (Canada)
10 Alcorn Avenue, Toronto, Ontario, Canada M4V 3B2
(a division of Pearson Penguin Canada Inc.)
Penguin Books Ltd
80 Strand, London WC2R 0RL, England
Penguin Ireland
25 St Stephen's Green, Dublin 2, Ireland
(a division of Penguin Books Ltd)
Penguin Books India Pvt Ltd
11 Community Centre, Panchsheel Park, New Delhi – 110 017, India
Penguin Group (NZ)
Cnr Airborne and Rosedale Roads, Albany, Auckland, New Zealand
(a division of Pearson New Zealand Ltd)
Penguin Books (South Africa) (Pty) Ltd
24 Sturdee Avenue, Rosebank, Johannesburg 2196, South Africa

Penguin Books Ltd, Registered Offices:
80 Strand, London, WC2R 0RL, England

First published by Penguin Group (Australia), a division of
Pearson Australia Group Pty Ltd, 2004

10 9 8 7 6 5 4 3 2 1

Design by Deborah Brash © Penguin Group (Australia)
Photography by David Matheson
Handwriting and drawings by David Band
Typeset in Univers by Post Pre-press Group, Brisbane, Queensland
Colour reproduction by Splitting Image Colour Studio Pty Ltd, Clayton, Victoria
Printed and bound in China through Bookbuilders

National Library of Australia
Cataloguing-in-Publication data:

Terzini, Maurizio.
Something Italian.

Includes index.
ISBN 1 920989 04 8.

1. Cookery, Italian. I. Title.

641.5945

www.penguin.com.au